MAURICE KENNY

MAURICE KENNY

Celebrations of a Mohawk Writer

EDITED BY

PENELOPE MYRTLE KELSEY

FOREWORD BY

JOSEPH BRUCHAC

STATE UNIVERSITY OF NEW YORK PRESS

Royalties from this collection will be donated to the Hiawatha Institute for Indigenous Knowledge.

Cover art "Maurice" (2002) by Nina Holland. Photo by Derek Maus.

Chapter 8 originally published as a review essay in *American Indian Culture and Research Journal* 18:1 (1994) 95–118.

Published by
State University of New York Press, Albany

Printed in the United States of America

For information, contact
State University of New York Press, Albany, NY
www.sunypress.edu

Production, Laurie Searl
Marketing, Fran Keneston

Library of Congress Cataloging-in-Publication Data

Maurice Kenny : celebrations of a Mohawk writer / edited by Penelope Myrtle Kelsey.
p. cm.
Includes bibliographical references and index.
ISBN 978-1-4384-3802-3 (pbk. : alk. paper)
ISBN 978-1-4384-3803-0 (hardcover : alk. paper)
1. Kenny, Maurice, 1929—-Criticism and interpretation. 2. Indians in literature. I. Kelsey, Penelope Myrtle.

PS3561.E49Z79 2011
811'.54—dc22 2011003236

10 9 8 7 6 5 4 3 2 1

To Levi and those yet unborn
whose faces are coming from beneath the ground.

CONTENTS

FOREWORD

"Maurice Kenny: Not Through Height"

Joseph Bruchac

There's a Nigerian proverb that I first heard while teaching in West Africa: "It is not through height that one sees the moon." But it was only when I first met my friend Maurice Kenny a few years after my return to the United States that I saw that wise saying embodied in the flesh.

I had published some of Maurice's poetry in our literary magazine, *The Greenfield Review*, before I met him in person at a poetry reading. My first impression was that this sharp-eyed, intense man with a gray ponytail was smaller than I had expected. Could he really be the author of such powerful, eloquent, impassioned poems as those published in the spring 1978 issue of our magazine where he had eulogized John Berryman in one, remembered the tragedy of Sand Creek in another, sung in a third Whitman-like lyric of the natural beauty of a threatened nature preserve in Long Island? He didn't seem to quite be a match for the power of his poems. That was, of course, before he began to read.

Maurice was not the only poet on the program, made up of three writers who had not read together previously. There was—as often happens at such events—some discussion about who was to go first. Neither of the other two writers (whose names shall go unmentioned) one wanted to be seen as the warm-up act. They nominated Maurice to lead off.

"Are you sure that you want me to go first?" Maurice said in a quiet voice, as I recall. "Oh, yes," was the reply. And then Maurice, a little smile on his face, replied "Alllll right."

Maurice took the stage, looked around at the audience, squared his shoulders, and began to read. To describe his voice as resonant and booming would be an understatement. Every eye was riveted on him as he seemed to swell in stature—like one of the changer heroes in our traditions who must confront some danger to the people and enlarges himself by speaking a word of power. When he finished and stepped quietly off the stage, there was an eloquent moment of awed silence before the thunder of applause. Everyone was moved, with the possible exception of the crestfallen next two readers. Talk about an impossible act to follow!

"See why I said I shouldn't go first," Maurice whispered as he sat down next to me. Then, straight-faced, we sat and listened attentively to the next two readers—unlike the large segment of the audience that departed after Maurice was done.

That night, which demonstrated both the gentlemanly and the assertive side of Maurice Kenny—as well as his subtle sense of humor—was, as one might say, the beginning of a beautiful friendship.

Of course, my love for Maurice is not just based on his ability as a reader, one as capable and charismatic as Dylan Thomas. There's no American author I can think of who, while always displaying a marvelous range of creative ability, had done more to encourage, teach, promote, and even publish other authors. A list of the Native writers he published is a literal who's who of American Indian writing in the last quarter of the twentieth century. I should add—as I know Maurice would want me to—that he also has encouraged and published many non-Indian writers. Maurice is truly an editor with a catholic (but not ecclesiastical) sensibility.

The essays in this collection bear witness to his ability to inspire others, his generosity of spirit, and the importance of his body of work as a significant part of the American literary canon. Note that I did not say "The American Indian literary canon." Maurice and I are unanimous in seeing American Indian literature as not merely some subset of American writing, but as a substantial part of American Literature—and World Literature—as a whole.

I have a great many memories of Maurice that are dear to me. One, is of him lugging boxes of books and magazines—his own work and that of the writers he was publishing through such ventures of his as Strawberry Press and Contact/II—from one book fair or reading to another. This after having had serious heart bypass surgery. And, more than once, when my wife Carol or I tried to take one of those boxes from him to lighten his load (taking note of the fact that his face was red and there were beads of sweat on his brow), his response was always "I've got it, Joe!" Maurice took it seriously when it came to supporting—literally—his own work and that of the people he brought out.

Another memory is from the time when he was about to abandon Brooklyn (after being brutally mugged in the hallway of his own apartment building). After he had visited us in Greenfield Center, Carol and I drove him one hundred miles further north during an intense winter storm. Finally, a mile or two from his destination, the road became impassable by car. When I cracked open the windows, we heard the wind howling like a pack of hungry wolves.

"We should go back," Carol suggested. But Maurice was already out the door.

"I'll walk from here," he said.

The last we saw of him (what we thought might in fact be the last that anyone saw of him!) was his determined back bent over as he disappeared in the swirling snow. But Maurice survived. Yet again. I won't go into this in detail, but I do not know of any poet who has had more close calls with mortality than Maurice. At one point, whenever I called him I found myself on the verge of starting every conversation with the questions, "So, what did you almost die of this time, Maurice?" Like his beloved cats, Maurice truly seems to have the proverbial nine lives.

I do not mean that in merely a joking way. Similar to some of the characters in our old tales, Maurice has gone through many changes in his life—while always remaining steadfastly focused on the literary life, his devotion to Iroquois history and heritage, and American Indian writing as a whole.

Maurice would move on from being an urban poet and publisher to the life of a successful and popular North Country college professor in far upstate New York. His students at North Country Community College (NCCC) and Paul Smith's College would find themselves as much in awe of his ability as a teacher of creative writing and literature as his audiences all around the country had been at his bardic brilliance behind a podium.

He also moved on from being a writer of lyric poetry to be the creator of great dramatic cycles around the lives the Jesuit priest Isaac Jogues and the powerful Mohawk woman leader Molly Brant. While continuing to be a prolific poet, he proved himself in further literary forms as an often anthologized writer of short stories, an insightful essayist.

And he never forgot the responsibility of serving the community. While Maurice was at NCCC a group of us—in which Maurice often was the first among equals—began to work to bring together what turned out to be a truly amazing major gathering of American Indian writers. Despite the fact that we had the support of Richard Margolies, a visionary social writer whose too brief life was devoted to the cause of equality, and the initial backing of The Bay Foundation, we still were far short of the support needed to pull it off. Many thought that it was an impossible task. But not Maurice, who arranged for NCCC to host our first major planning meeting and was as energetic in support of our quest as the Energizer Rabbit! That we were able to bring together more than three hundred American Indian writers in Norman, Oklahoma in July 1992, many of them at the start of their careers, and subsidize their travel, food and lodging for the event, was nothing short of a miracle. And there was no one who deserved more credit for its success than Maurice.

There are so many more stories I could relate about Maurice. I'm not alone in that. I'm sure that virtually everyone he published, everyone who published him, everyone who shared a stage with him or heard him read has at least one memorable Maurice Kenny story. Not all of them may be pleasant. Kind as he is, Maurice has never suffered fools gladly. There can be iron as well as irony in his voice. He's never been afraid to speak truth to power, to put his life on the line.

It is good that there is much more about Maurice Kenny and his work in the pages that follow these peripatetic musings of mine. They do some justice to him, to what I see as a lasting human and literary legacy.

What would be best of all, what I wish could be preserved through the ages, is Maurice himself. But I suppose his writing and the writing about him and the recordings of his presentations will have to be enough.

May our grandchildren know him.

ACKNOWLEDGMENTS

Thanks to the many individuals who made the publication of this book possible. Thanks to Cheryl Savageau, Siobhan Senier, and Lisa Brooks for their encouragement to pursue this project in its earliest stages and for their sage advice regarding the endeavor as a whole. Thanks to the Haudenosaunee scholars, writers, artists, clanmothers, and chiefs, and to the Two-Spirit/LGBTQ scholars, writers, artists, and individuals who have come before us in this project. Thanks to the Department of English of the Rochester Institute of Technology, the English & Journalism Department of Western Illinois University, and the English Department of the University of Colorado at Boulder for their support in the long-term creation and editing of this collection.

ONE

READING THE WAMPUM

An Introduction to the Works of Maurice Kenny

Penelope Myrtle Kelsey

In 1929 in Cape Vincent, a small burg near the industrial behemoth of Watertown, New York, Maurice Kenny was born to Anthony Andrew Kenny and Doris Marie Parker Herrick Kenny, a Mohawk/Irish father and Seneca/English mother. His beginning was not particularly noteworthy, although he never lacked for anything as a child, but his birthplace would infinitely determine his future. In their silent (and sometimes noisy) ways, the Adirondacks woods and mountains were leaving their imprint on the young Kenny, as he spent his youth fishing their streams, working their fields, and berrying their clearings. Forty years later in a Brooklyn loft, Kenny would turn to the North Country and his Mohawk roots, taking up the pen to put Native American experience to paper, and this new era of his life would generate an ouevre of work that represents a generation and captures Indigenous existence like no other writer.

In his poetry and fiction, Maurice Kenny celebrates berries, bears, and bloodroot, all images of the Adirondacks and the Mohawk way of life: these are the sources to which Louise Bogan urged Kenny to turn. "Write what you know," insisted Bogan, and Kenny responded. Kenny portrays Kanien'keha (Mohawk) encounters with early colonialists and renarrates stories untold in print from a Native American perspective. He painfully examines the losses incumbent on the Iroquois, from the slash-and-burn campaign of Sullivan and Clinton to the current contamination of the waters at Akwesasne, the same waters celebrated in the Thanksgiving Address and the living environment of fish, once a staple of the traditional Kanien'keha diet. Kenny excoriates the brutal capitalist processes that consume Indigenous territories and peoples, and he draws the connections between Turtle Island and the larger global South. The strawberries brought to Kenny in his hospital bed in 1974 after a near fatal heart infection were picked by Mayan and Aztec farm workers in Mexico and shipped from their expropriated hands to Brooklyn. Kenny keenly sees and articulates these cosmopolitan and diasporic connections, as evidenced in his biography of Frida Kahlo (in press) and his collaboration with authors like Lorna Cervantes.

Kenny has contributed tremendously to the growth of multicultural literatures of North American in his work as an editor for Contact II Press and as a mentor to emerging writers of color. The profound impact of this work on writers from Eric Gansworth and Wendy Rose to Lorna Cervantes and Diane Burns profoundly changed the face of U.S. ethnic literatures as we know it. Kenny's circle has included luminaries like Allen Ginsberg, Amiri Baraka, Jerome Rothenberg, Audre Lorde, and Carolyn Forché. In his years of "Greyhounding" America and giving readings in venues from bookstores and universities to coffeehouses and tribal colleges, Kenny sometimes gave as many as one hundred readings in a year, and in this capacity, his all-encompassing identity as a Mohawk orator is clearest. Abenaki poet and longtime friend Joseph Bruchac has glossed Kenny's performative repertoire as an act of "reading the wampum," and even audience members unfamiliar with Haudenosaunee oratory are struck by Kenny's resonant, booming voice, his careful turn of phrase, and his use of the physical body as a tool in delivery. Kenny's gift to literature of the turn of the century has been both sweeping and universal, detailed and local.

BIOGRAPHY

From his early days in Cape Vincent, Maurice Kenny took powerful images of the North Country land, infusing them with scents, colors, and textures of chicory, hawkweed, and pearly everlasting. Few of Kenny's poems escape this signature mark of respect for the land embodied in a storied presence of its seasonal changes and momentary details. The lessons Kenny learned from the elders around him, his Aunt Jenny as well as his father, began his cultural training as Mohawk and encouraged his nascent poet's eye. Kenny's engagement of the North Country as a poetic tapestry that is at once a setting for all the poet explores as well as the same land occupied and guarded by the Kanien'kehaka creates a range of expression and a sense of history that few other writers can match.

These early years also brought tremendous pain, as Kenny reflects in *Angry Rain: A Brief Autobiographical Memoir from Boyhood to College*:

> William Faulkner, the Mississippi novelist, once wrote that we must be violated by life. The Lakota Holy Man black Elk once said that we human beings must celebrate the greening of the day. I have celebrated that green spring and flowery summer, that russet autumn and snowy January. I have also been violated, and in turn violated life. The violation and the celebration have produced hundreds of poems and stories and made me acquainted with the night, the day, and more human beings than I can possibly remember.[1]

Taking the excruciating pain of boyhood assaults and attacks, Kenny later reformulates them into a brutal sensuality and foreboding sexuality that pervade *Isaac Jogues*, *Molly Brant*, and *Connotations*. This view into the darker side of human nature adds a depth to Kenny's portrayal of colonialism that leaves the reader without question of its cruelty and lack of humanity.

These early years also were characterized by Kenny's strong desire for fame as exemplified by the fortune teller who once told his mother that he would be tremendously famous *and* that she saw him surrounded by books . . . or stones. She claimed he might not see fame in his own lifetime, but that he would surely be famous. This prediction inspired Kenny and determined the direction of much of his early efforts, leading to wild days skipping school and riding the subway into Manhattan to collect signatures from movie stars like Orson Welles and Rita Hayworth.

At eighteen, three years after his parents' separation and one year after an ill-fated trip to the deep South, during which he would be abducted, bound, and sexually assaulted by a stranger in the Mississippi swamp, Kenny began attending Butler University in Indianapolis, where he was mentored by poet Ray Marz and Werner Beyer. Kenny so adored his years at Butler that when his graduation approached and he was faced with returning to upstate New York, he suffered a nervous breakdown, necessitating his sister and brother-in-law driving across the United States to bring him home. In these years, Kenny published his first collections of poetry, *The Hopeless Kill* (1956), *Dead Letters Sent and Other Poems* (1958), *With Love to Lesbia* (1959), and *And Grieve, Lesbia* (1960); these books were impressed by Kenny's traditional training at Butler and did not reflect his burgeoning Mohawk identity in any overt way. During this time he lived in New York City, Mexico, the Virgin Islands, and Chicago alternately until his move to Brooklyn in the late 1960s. Kenny now turned more seriously to his craft, beginning a master's program at the City University with Louise Bogan and rejecting the free tuition his father offered him to attend Columbia. With Bogan's guidance and the American Indian Community House artistic milieu, Kenny's writing turned to Indigenous New York themes. His most dramatic moment of awakening, however, occurred during the Wounded Knee Occupation of 1973, when Kenny was immobilized on bedrest as a result of a heart condition. Kenny recounts his tremendous sense of frustration at not being able to join Pine Ridge community members and American Indian Movement activists or support them through working with Jerry Campbell and other Mohawks at *Akwesasne Notes*. Kenny says, "I was sick. There's no two ways about it . . . because of the traveling [to give readings] and going to reservations and meeting people. What I had in my mind [when composing *I Am the Sun*] was what I know about my land and my people, I can take out to other lands, and what I have learned from those people [other Native Americans] I can bring back" (Interview 2/8/2003). As a direct response to being confined to bedrest at such a pivotal political juncture, Kenny published *I Am the Sun* (1976), a poetic revision of the Lakota Sundance.

This collection was soon followed by a rapid succession of chapbooks: *North: Poems of Home* (1977), *Dancing Back Strong the Nation* (1979), *Only as Far as Brooklyn* (1981), *Kneading the Blood* (1981), *Boston Tea Party* (1982), *The Smell of Slaughter* (1982), and *Blackrobe* (1982). Both *Blackrobe* and *Between Two Rivers* (1987) were nominated for Pulitzer Prizes, and in 1984, Kenny was awarded the prestigious American Book Award for *The Mama Poems*, a memoir about his mother, who died in a housefire in 1982. The succession of poetry collections continues with *Is Summer This Bear* (1985), *Greyhounding This America* (1988), *Humors And / Or Not So Humorous* (1988), *The Short and the Long of It* (1990), *Last Mornings in Brooklyn* (1991), *Tekonwatonti: Molly Brant* (1992), *On Second Thought* (1995), *Common Days: A Place Record* (1998), *In the Time of the Present* (2000), *Carving Hawk: New and Selected Poems* (2002), and *Connotations* (2008). An ambitious writer, Kenny has never been restricted by genre, publishing two collections of fiction, *Rain and Other Fictions* (1985) and *Tortured Skins* (2000), and two prose collections, *On Second Thought* (1995) and *Backward to Forward* (1997). Beyond this publication list lie nearly one hundred journal publications, numerous edited projects, and several unpublished manuscripts.

Kenny has held numerous residencies at universities, tribal colleges, First Nations centers in Canada and the United States, and the Oneida Nation of Wisconsin. Kenny was awarded an honorary doctorate by St. Lawrence University in 1995 and the Elder Achievement Award by the Wordcraft Circle of Native Writers in 2000. He served on the board of directors for numerous foundations including the New York Foundation for the Arts and the Coordinating Council of Literary Magazines, and he organized significant gatherings of Native American writers including Returning the Gift in Norman, Oklahoma and the Iroquois Arts Festival and Native American Women's Festival in Saranac Lake.

CRITICISM

Although there exists an extensive record of interviews of Maurice Kenny, only a small body of literary criticism has been published, amounting to four articles in scholarly journals and short reviews of his works. This collection, thus, fills a significant need to examine the work of this preeminent Native poet. Because Kenny has been so influential in other artists' craft, this collection is divided into two sections, one devoted to creative writers' musings on Kenny's influence and a second section devoted to traditional critical essays. In the first section, "Creative Responses," Eric Gansworth recounts his first meeting with Maurice Kenny as a neophyte author in "You, Too, Will Have This Printed Word (World) of Your Own." Gansworth's essay highlights the profound impact of Kenny's mentoring, a kind of relationship that Kenny has recreated many times over with authors from numerous tribal backgrounds and creative writing students at institutions from British Columbia to New York. Mohawk poet James Stevens contributes the second essay in "Creative Responses," entitled "The Breath and Skin of History," a meditation upon artistic process and renarrating histories. Stevens' *A Bridge Dead in the Water* considers many of the same historical figures as Kenny's *Blackrobe*, and Stevens examines the unique position of the Mohawk writer writing back to the *Jesuit Relations*. Qwo-Li Driskill, an emerging Tsalagi poet and Two-Spirit critic, focuses on the demands on Indigenous activist praxis that Kenny's poetry articulates in the essay, "Dancing Strong Our Nations: Performance as Continuance in Maurice Kenny's Poetry." Examining performance as a rhetorical device in Kenny's poetry, Driskill asserts that Kenny's work offers a model from which Native peoples can create art that aids in the continuance and survival of Native communities and nations.

The second section, "Critical Engagements," begins with Susan Ward's repositioning of a question Lance Henson once asked Kenny, "How Can Any Self-Respecting Mohawk Live in a Place Like Brooklyn?" Ward's response depends on the always already Iroquois nature of the five boroughs, which have long been inhabited by week-day commuters from the numerous Mohawk communities in northern New York and southern Ontario and Quebec; she also discusses the nature of the impact of Mohawk steelworkers on this Indigenous flavor of New York City. D/Lakota scholar Nicholle Dragone's essay, "*Tortured Skins*, Bears, and Humankind's Obligations and Responsibilities to the Natural World," provides a deeply culturally situated investigation of Haudenosaunee *ohkwa:ri* or bear images in Kenny's second fiction collection. Dragone establishes ample cultural context for understanding bears in the Kanien'keha worldview and insightfully discusses the seven stories in *Tortured Skins* that imagine bears as a proving ground for the relevance of the Thanksgiving Address to contemporary Native and non-Native life. In "Teaching Maurice Kenny's Fiction: Dislocated Characters, Narrators, and Readers," Karen Gibson and Alan Steinberg consider the challenges of teaching Kenny's fictional narratives in the non-Native classroom. They read various stories from *Tortured Skins* against the historical backdrop of exploration and contemporary environmental depredations, suggesting Kenny's formal strategies alienate the reader from the normalizing of the settler culture's destruction of Native peoples and their lands. In his review essay for *Tekonwatonti*, Craig Womack details the clanmother identity of Molly Brant in Kenny's work and outlines a psychoanalytic reading of Brant and William Johnson as figures of Kenny's own parents. In "Painting 'Word-Pictures' in Place: Maurice Kenny's Empathetic Imagination of *Tekonwatonti / Molly Brant*," Abenaki cultural historian Lisa Brooks argues for a reassessment of Kenny's work as a critical Northeastern woodland response to the colonizing forces of dominant understandings of history and Indian identity. She maintains that in *Tekonwatonti* Kenny creates "word-pictures" or "word-paintings" that communicate in glyphs similarly to wampum, revealing connections between Haudenosaunee materials records, oral tradition, and Kenny's poetic voice. In the final essay, " 'Dancing Back Strong the Nation': Two-Spirit Images in the Work of Maurice Kenny," Lisa Tatonetti excavates and addresses the long pattern of lesbian, gay, bisexual, transgender, and queer (LGBTQ) themes in Kenny's opus from its inception to present, laying the groundwork for future investigations of a Two-Spirit sensibility particularly in Kenny's imitative, yet innovative, early poetry collections.

The goal of this collection is to examine the work of a vital contributor to the American Indian literary scene in the second half of the twentieth century and the first half of the twenty-first century. Although sometimes published in small, independent presses, Kenny's work has withstood the test of time, and the accolades he has won from corners as far removed as the Wordcraft Circle of Native Writers to National Public Radio attest to the breadth and vision of his imaginings of Indian survival in the new millennium. We offer our praise and give the Creator thanks for the opportunity to honor our elder.

NOTE

1. Kenny, Maurice. "Angry Rain: A Brief Autobiographical Memoir from Boyhood to College," *Contemporary Authors Autobiography Series* 22 (1995): 122.

TWO

YOU, TOO, WILL HAVE THIS PRINTED WORD (WORLD) OF YOUR OWN

Eric Gansworth

Maurice Kenny has the most inscrutable, yet elegant handwriting. It looks somewhat like glyph work, and fifteen years into our friendship, I often still have to guess on some words when reading a letter from him. My own handwriting, as my students will attest, is no easy read either, and I suspect they often cope with my comments the way I do with Maurice's correspondence: filling in the blanks, sometimes perhaps to suit their own needs. This mechanism grows easier the longer you know someone. You can hear that person's voice, anticipate their chain of logic and the lens through which they see the world. When you first see someone's handwriting, however, it's still a mystery.

In spring 1992, I ran into Tuscarora photographer and art historian Jolene Rickard for the first time in a formal setting at an event I had organized, bringing Ted Williams to speak to students with whom I was working. When we spoke, she handed me a pamphlet concerning the first comprehensive conference of Indigenous writers, "Returning the Gift," scheduled for July of that year, the quincentenary of colonialism on this continent. I have no idea how she knew at the time that I was writing. I had completed one terrible horror novel that will never see publication and two short stories that were actually viable.

Jolene urged me to attend the conference, and I clarified that the job I had was a twelve-month appointment, and that I did not have the money to pay for the gathering. She asked me how serious I was about writing. It was an open-ended question with lots of interpretive doors trailing out beyond it. I replied that I was pretty serious. She wrote down a phone number and urged me to call this person to discuss my potential travel support.

The person was Maurice Kenny. I had read his work in an anthology I had and maybe a few poems in journals. From his biography, I knew he was somebody whose work I should have been more familiar with than I was. At the time, he was the author of more than eighteen books of poetry and fiction. He had won an American Book Award, the Hodson Prize, and the National Public Radio Broadcasting Award, among a number of other significant awards. Writers to me were these ethereal beings, living in a world I only dreamed of, and Maurice's impressive career certainly reflected that life. He had been dedicated enough to his craft that he had garnered among the most significant awards in the country. I was painfully aware of my own ignorance and woefully minimal credentials, as I picked up the telephone to introduce myself to Maurice. To my surprise, he was expecting my call.

He explained the regretful situation fairly quickly, which was that I was in too strange a place for financial assistance to attend the conference. I was no longer a student, so there were no scholarships for which I qualified. I also had not yet had anything published, so professional travel funds were also closed to me. He did offer that if I found a way to make it to Oklahoma, materials would be waiting for me, that the conference fees would be waived. We talked briefly about the possibility of my being one of the readers, and he said we would have to wait and see. Then he turned the conversation immediately to writing.

What Maurice did in that simple gesture was to treat me as a writer and to talk about craft and career. I understood that although he was not in a position to offer me financial assistance, he opened a door and, in some ways, like Jolene, forced the question: how serious was I? It was April, and I sat in a small upstairs room thinking. The sharp spring air trailed into the window, cracked open after a winter of being sealed, as we talked about writing like two professionals who had known each other for years. At the end of the conversation, he asked me to mail him some of my work.

How serious about writing was I? At the time, I was teaching as an adjunct at two colleges, writing when I could, and, bizarrely, had found that I had gotten a full-time job at a nearby university, as a mentor and student advocate of sorts to Indigenous students in a graduate program. I was relatively unqualified for the job, but I did have the most important one for the sustenance of the program's funding: I was an enrolled member of an Indigenous nation. It turned out to be one of the clichés of Indian life, the token job. I was in a professional position I did not like, where I was paid a fairly decent salary to do almost nothing, and where my efforts to perform advocacy were met with suspicion and accusation. I had decorated my office with one of my paintings, and a person involved in the program insisted that the students said it represented a bad omen. The same person claimed my preference for natural light through open windows instead of the fluorescent ceiling lights created a hostile environment that was full of shadows and foreboding.

My supervisor at one point informed me that I was not doing my best to fit in with preexisting personalities. I asked if this also had been true of the three previous Indigenous people who had held the position. She replied that they had had issues of their own, and that I had to decide if I enjoyed having a stable income. After two months in the position, spurred on by Maurice's treatment of me as an actual professional at something I aspired to be, I resigned. Concerned that federal Indian funding might be jeopardized with an emerging pattern in which the only Indian employees rapidly departed, all stemming from their having "had issues of their own," the supervisor tried to convince me that I could not walk away from a decent paying job with no plans, which turned out to be wrong on both accounts. I could walk away. I also had plans.

Without funding and with the temporary pay of an adjunct salary, I was forced to decide if making my way to Oklahoma would be important enough to use up critical resources. I decided that it was. With the committed help and support of a friend with a van, I hit the road. I took very few things with me: some changes of clothes, a manuscript of my terrible horror novel, and a couple of short stories I had recently polished that were much more literary in their qualities. I also brought one book with me: the recently published anthology, *Talking Leaves*.

I stumbled on this anthology of contemporary American Indian fiction the year before. Ultimately, it was interchangeable with several others that had come out at the same time, and in that period, I was walking around almost wholly in the dark. I knew the work of a few other Indian writers, such as Ted C. Williams, Louise Erdrich, Thomas King, Leslie Marmon Silko, Joy Harjo, and N. Scott Momaday, but that was it. I had gone through a bachelor's and a master's in English having read two things for class that would have been considered American Indian literature: Silko's "Yellow Woman" and the speech of Seattle. This was the time just before multiculturalism really took off in the classroom or at least multiculturalism that included Indian voices. Whatever American Indian literature I read came my way with luck or with the assistance and suggestions of others, rather than through any formal program of study.

I had recently discovered that my skills as a writer were proficient enough that I could sustain the narrative of a novel and was working on a second. When I found this anthology, I picked it up, figuring I should know the work of as many people as possible who were doing the same thing I was attempting. I recognized some of the names, but there was a significant number I did not. I was humbled by the number of terrific writers who had come before me, and was inspired by their work to one day join them, if

I were committed to the possibility. This anthology was a crash course in contemporary Indian writers. What I was learning most from the anthology was that I knew almost nothing. It had been my guide the year before, so I decided to bring it along for the trip.

After trekking south, taking in a Charlie Daniels concert in Nashville, catching a surreal show of a white woman dressed up and singing like Tina Turner in an Opryland stage show, crossing the Mississippi for the first time, and witnessing numerous dead armadillos in the blistering flatness of Arkansas, I stepped into the large building on the University of Oklahoma campus in Norman. Hit by the almost frigid temperature contrasting the outside, I wandered to the registration table to find my materials waiting, as Maurice said they would be. He had made good on his promise. I had no idea, walking into this enormous room full of Indians a few minutes later for the conference welcome, even what Maurice looked like. Beyond the twenty or so people whose work I had read in that anthology, hundreds of writers filled the lecture hall, and we all knew as we gathered there, that we were a part of something new, unprecedented, and remarkable.

I sat among one of the last rows, getting close to some other people, so that it might appear that I was attending with someone. Fortunately, they did not notice me or ask me to move on. I kept watch on nametags as discreetly as possible, which is never easy to accomplish. As luck would have it, however, one of the people I had been sitting near yelled out "Maurice" and I turned to see a slight man with a silver ponytail turn, eyebrows raised. He and the man who had spoken his name caught up with some brief business. When he finished, I too called his name and introduced myself. He was clearly rushing off, as he was constantly inundated with questions as a conference organizer, but he stopped to welcome me and ask me how my travel had been and if I had gotten registered. I assured him everything was fine, and asked if he had thought my work was good enough to be involved in the readings. He informed me that I had sent him interesting work, and also that the professional readings were booked straight through the conference, but he did offer to set me up in one of the afternoon student readings.

This response was naturally not the one I had hoped for, but I also had been around long enough to understand hierarchy and thanked him for the opportunity. Much of what I recall about the conference is fragmentary after all these years. I remember meeting Alex Jacobs after having been mistaken for him a couple of times, and hearing LeAnne Howe light the night on fire with her reading. I met a few people who were friendly and with whom I comfortably hung around. I did run into a couple of people I knew. Jolene was there, photographing many of the events in a professional capacity. She seemed to know everyone and introduced me to quite a few people.

Ted Williams also was there. One incredibly sweaty night, at the end of the evening's readings, I ran into Ted as we left the lobby and asked him where he was staying. He said, "all the writers are staying at The Sooner House," and then he paused and continued, "I'd sooner being staying some place where it wasn't 104 degrees at eleven at night." We laughed, and it was sort of like home. But as I drove back to the campground outside of town where my friend and I were staying, his words stuck with me. I had driven more than one thousand miles to be at the gathering, but I was still not one of the writers.

The day of the student readings, Maurice showed up to make sure I was indeed on the list and introduced me to the moderator. Among the other student readers was Penny Olson, and she was overcome, reading her story aloud. It was a very difficult story, one I would not have been brave enough to write or read as my own at such a young age. She told me afterward that the editor had accepted it for the "Doubleday Anthology" that a lot of people were talking about. It was possible to rise from student to writer, even through the course of these few days, but it did not happen to me there. I was going to leave the conference still not officially a writer.

I am the sort of person who accrues mementos, and when I stepped into that building the first day, the one thing I brought with me in my backpack was that original anthology I had found and had dragged across the country, determined to get it signed by as many of the contributors as I met. In the end, I had fewer than ten people sign it, being too shy to approach most of the people I recognized. When I planned to approach someone, friends of theirs often would come flying out of nowhere, rejoicing in their reunions, and I did not want to intrude on those lives. As years went on, I eventually had a couple more people sign it, but then stopped because in some ways, it had inadvertently become an artifact of that conference. Of the other writers I have had the opportunity to meet since then, I have largely had them sign copies of their books, and have left my first Indian literature anthology on the shelf.

Occasionally, I pick this book up and flip through it to read the inscriptions, as one might with an old high school yearbook. A number of people gave straight, plain signatures, and others offered neutral pleasantries, "best wishes," and "nice to meet you," but Maurice spent a bit of time thinking about what he was going to write and then handed it back to me satisfied. I have always found it awkward to read an inscription at the time of the person's writing, so I generally wait until we have parted company before I read them. Among the good wishes from the other writers, Maurice's was different. He wrote, "You, too, will have this printed word of your own," or maybe he wrote, "You, too, will have this printed *world* of your own." All these years later, I still can't tell. Both seem equally appropriate.

It was midway through the conference, and I was glad I had asked him when I did. He departed early, and I don't think I saw him after he had signed it. We have never discussed his early departure, but from what

I understand, he was troubled by the behavior of a young writer that he had nurtured and that he had not been able to help in the capacity he had hoped.

I understand his dilemma these days, having failed in some attempts to help others and even wondering if I had failed those students in the job I had left. If I had been a better or stronger advocate, might I have made their lives easier? It's hard to say. As far as I know, they have all reached their promise, and I hope they understood that I left in part because I had been unsuccessful in doing what I had been hired to do: to advocate for them within their program.

I discussed my departure with one of them shortly before I made the decision, and the student told me that the program was the most important thing in life and that if I made a decision that required the taking of sides, the student was going to side with my supervisor. I might have been the only Indian staff member, but the supervisor was the only person who could facilitate a successful navigation through the system. We both understood the reality that our lives lay along separate paths, and I alone understood that mine would shortly lead me to a blistering summer in Oklahoma, full of hope.

I didn't get "discovered," as I had hoped, during the course of that conference Maurice had been instrumental in organizing. I also didn't get into the anthology published to celebrate the occasion of the conference. I submitted materials, according to the guidelines, but found out later it was really for "invited participants only." In the months that followed, however, I ran into people who had been there, when they came to read in western New York: Joy Harjo, Diane Glancy, and Beth Brant. In most cases, we had not met on the physical grounds of the University of Oklahoma, but we had the shared history Maurice had facilitated in his generosity, and this shared history opened the door of generosity and did lead me in the direction of my first publication. I had a story accepted in an anthology by that fall, and it was set to be published in the summer.

Two months before the story was to be released, I saw that Maurice was scheduled to read in Buffalo at the established literary center where I had done a couple of workshops in American Indian literature in the fall, largely based on that same anthology. I called their offices to see if the opening slot had been filled already, still so new at this profession that I was entirely unaware of how inappropriate my call had been and that this was not the way one went about establishing a relationship. To their credit, they politely said that they indeed already had someone lined up for the position. I thanked them and hung up, wondering who it would be.

A day later, the center called me back, saying they had reconsidered and would like me to read in the opening slot, and they offered me an honorarium to do so. I happily accepted, believing I was successfully raising my profile and that this was merely a sign of things to come. On the evening of the reading, standing outside in the warm June air of Buffalo, waiting for Maurice to arrive, I asked the director what circumstances had brought about this change of heart or if the initial reader had backed out. She said she had spoken with Maurice and that he had insisted I open for him and that I be paid as any other writer would have been paid. She had expressed reservations because I had not yet technically published anything. Maurice had somehow known my story would be out shortly. Again, I have no idea how he does it, but he seems even now to keep track of beginning writers who could use some support. He told her that she would not regret giving me my first shot at a reading. He was in the process of helping make his cryptic inscription come true.

I would like to think that I was somehow special and that Maurice had merely recognized what should have been evident, but his friendship and mentorship in my case merely reflected the key role as early advocate and publisher he has had for many American Indian writers. In addition to his undisputed talent as an award-winning writer, he is known almost as universally for his generosity. The first time I stayed at Maurice's place, after an Indian writers festival he had organized in Saranac Lake, we sat in his kitchen and drank coffee, and I noticed all the signed books and drawings and paintings surrounding us throughout his house.

I have been back a number of times in subsequent years, and he has stayed at my place when he reads in Buffalo, a small return I have offered for his thoughtfulness. I know that a number of promising writers he helped have, for whatever reason, not been able to sustain consistent careers in the pursuit, and I hope that he understands the key role he played in the formative stages of my career. Each time I've returned to his home, I've noticed how it continues to fill with the artifacts of his own generosity of spirit, coming back in gratitude. In each case, there were acknowledgments, confirming I was merely a recent entry in a long list of people he had granted that talismanic good wish, his belief that we, too, would have this printed word (world) of our own.

THREE

THE BREATH AND SKIN OF HISTORY

James Thomas Stevens

It is impossible to be a Kanien'keha writer, or Haudenosaunee for that matter, without having an awareness of the works of Maurice Kenny. Kenny, like the long line of great Haudenosaunee orators before him, is a tireless recorder of not only Iroquois history, but of sorrows, joys, and atrocities that Native peoples have collectively experienced. By giving voice in poetic form to those who have come before us, he recreates an Indigenous perspective; his aim is historical reckoning.

This history and often the shocking lack of its record, the lacuna of our voices, of Indian voices, is the driving force behind the poetry of Maurice Kenny. Whether in the purely historical series, such as *Blackrobe* and *Tekonwatonti*, or the poetic musings inspired by history as in "Sand Creek, Colorado," where Kenny's recurring lament is summed-up in the lines, "the state marker says nothing / of the women, the children / or White Antelope's cry . . ."—one can be sure that history *will* be recorded.[1]

I first became aware of Maurice Kenny's writing in the late 1980s. I had moved to New York City from rural western New York State. My grandparents were living on the Tuscarora Nation in Lewiston, with my parents and a handful of other Mohawk relatives living just seven miles north in Youngstown. It was a big move from a town of two thousand to the borough of Brooklyn, and I quickly sought out a Native community, attending powwows at the McBirney YMCA and the American Indian Community House on Broadway. I took a job with the Museum of the American Indian—Gustave Heye Collection, then located at 155th and Broadway. It was while working there that I had the good fortune of coming across Maurice's thin 1982 poetry collection, *The Smell of Slaughter*.

I was an excited nineteen-year-old, excited to find a Mohawk poet who had grown up with same smells, sounds and imagery that I carried with me into that city—the imagery of small towns and hunters, cattails and river ice, corn, beans, and squash. Moving into the urban world would change that imagery, as I would discover it had changed the imagery of Maurice Kenny. I sought out Maurice's work and found that he too had moved to Brooklyn; he had adapted, as (almost all) urban Indians do, adaptability always our strength.

I would follow Maurice's work over the years, from *Only as Far as Brooklyn*, through *Is Summer This Bear* and *Last Mornings in Brooklyn*, all the way through to *In the Time of the Present*. No matter whether Kenny was documenting his own emotions and experiences in Brooklyn and while "greyhounding" across America, or the mysterious political murder of Annie-Mae Aquash, what he was recording were the experiences of present day Natives. These are the experiences that desperately need to be heard.

In the past century, when non-Native editors decided to put together anthologies of Native American work, they wanted only the traditional "pristine-Native" stories, accounts of Indians "unchanged and unspoiled" by the coming of Europeans. Often, eastern Native writers were overlooked, as they had forcibly adapted to their changing world since the early days of the encounter. The story of the ironworking Indian struggling in the Great Lakes cities, was not "Indian" enough. The stories of Native people surviving the christianizing process, while fighting to hold onto tradition, lost out to stories of buffalo hunts, sun dances, war parties, and Native lore. Maurice's poems resist this prescribed identity. He speaks of the reality of being Native in the, now, twenty-first century.

Kenny's 1988 poem, "Oroville High, California," speaks directly to this desire to record, and more specifically to society's shocking obliviousness to its necessity. The poem is presumably written after a visit to the California high school's print shop, in the town where Ishi appeared in 1911, alone and destitute, the sole survivor of his band of Yahis. Surveyors had spotted the band of four in 1908, but by 1911, Ishi was the only one alive. Butchers found Ishi outside of a slaughterhouse, but they were unable to communicate with him. Ishi was the last speaker of the Yahi dialect, a subgroup of the Yana. In fact, Ishi, is not even his name; we will never know that. The word, Ishi, is simply the word for *man* in the Yana dialect, and was given to him by University of California Berkeley anthropologist, Alfred Kroeber.

Ishi would spend the next five years living in the Berkeley anthropology museum, with a brief time in 1915 at the home of anthropologist Thomas Talbot Waterman. He was billed as the "last wild Indian in North America, a man of Stone Age culture," and he would suffer much-publicized cultural experiments, like sending him out for a night on the town with a high-class society lady. Anthropologists sought to find out all they could about this "wonderful specimen," and upon locating a California Native who spoke a related dialect, they were able to ask Ishi from where he came. Ishi would speak straight through for hours on end, beginning with the birth of the natural world, and he would fill countless wax recording cylinders with his story.

It is here that Maurice Kenny speaks to Ishi's desperate recounting of his origin and laments sets in opposition the complete the print shop students' disregard for even their own histories:

> They're ambivalent to instruction,
> indifferent to machines which will record
> their births and local football games . . .
> machines which are indifferent to Oroville
> itself, the buttes beyond the town's
> rigid limits where Ishi clawed rock desperately
> struggling to preserve his unrecorded songs.[2]

Kenny ends the poem with the image of students that not only do not know or care about the history of their own town, not the almond groves nor the gold, "let alone / Ishi's drum, nor the crisis of extermination, / not even their own."[3]

It is this desire to record, to leave a mark, to say, "I was here. I existed. I felt," that drives individuals—the artist to paint / sculpt the lasting image, the poet to write. It drives not only the creative force, but also the procreative force—births to ensure continuation. Which of us doesn't long to leave the mark of being? And for individuals belonging to culturally threatened or once decimated communities / tribes / cultures, this desire becomes imperative. We were / are here. You will hear our stories.

History without voice is pure academic knowledge. It is the place of the poet to give history voice, personae, to make us consider the human and not just the historical player. Early post-contact Iroquois history is intertwined with the lives of the French who arrived in Upper Canada. Of particular note is the brotherhood of the Jesuits or "Blackrobes" in what is now, Quebec, Ontario and New York State. Their influence and effect on Mohawk peoples in particular was significant.

Having just returned from a trip up to the North Country, up to Akwesasne, this influence is clearer than ever in my mind. In walking through the cemetery, searching for my great-grandmother, Hattie Cook Bero's, grave, I passed by countless Bonapartes, LaFrances, Papineaus, Arquettes (pronounced ar-kwit there) and Jacques (now become Jock). I traveled out to Kanatakon at the mouth of the Saint Regis River to the old stone Jesuit church. Above the door is a stained glass window depicting a blackrobe preaching to Saint Kateri Tekakwitha, and a statue of her stands watch across the street in the rectory garden—a symbol of the success of the Jesuit missionaries and martyrs.

My own interest in the lives of "the eight northern martyrs" came somewhat recently. Martyrdoms always interested me in the visual arts, their strange blending of agony and ecstasy, and as my poetic work became more and more about working with historical texts due to the beauty and strangeness of their language, it wasn't long before I found myself spending hours behind the pages of *The Jesuit Relations*. My brother, Scott Manning Stevens, director of the D'Arcy McNickle Center for American Indian and Indigenous Studies at the Newberry Library, is a seventeenth-century scholar, focusing on the literature of the encounter, and his appreciation of Jesuit literature provided an impetus for my research as well.

While working on my series of Jesuit poems, *A Species of Martyrdom: The Huronia Series*, I resisted looking at Maurice Kenny's *Blackrobe* collection. I would also come across a book of poems by Eldon Garret called, *Brebeuf: A Martyrdom of Jean De*, in a Toronto used bookstore. I would resist this too, as I wanted to keep my focus purely my own. That focus was on the strangely erotic element of the accounts. Immediately evident is the priests' strong desire to not only die in the name of Christ, but to die with very specific brethren. In the case of Jean de Lalande, he got his wish to be killed alongside Isaac Jogues, while Noël Chabanel would lament having missed the opportunity to be martyred with Jogues, even in a land "so fertile in palms and crowns."

I impatiently awaited the chance to read Kenny's *Blackrobe* poems, and upon finishing my own series I quickly delved into them. I was fascinated with how quickly human Isaac Jogues became. Even though Jogues was quite capable of writing and did so eloquently in the *Jesuit Relations*, Kenny's short poetic form and concise language allow for a clearer version due to a thinning out of religious rhetoric. What is perhaps most valuable in Kenny's poems is giving voice to the Native people who were affected by mission, people like Kiosaeton, Wolf Aunt, Kateri Tekakwitha, and the People of the Flint (Mohawks) themselves.

It is at the ecstatic / erotic intersection of my own reading of *The Jesuit Relations* with Kenny's that I must be most critical. Although it is my belief that the love shared between the Jesuit brothers, understandably when alone in the New World and in an order exclusively male, often crossed a kind of (homo)erotic threshold, I believe that Kenny's particular queering of the text is unsubstantiated. *The Relations* are full of passages such as the following, where Jogues describes the appearance of his priestly brother, René Goupil, after a torturing by the Iroquois, ". . . nothing white appeared in his face except his eyes. I found him all the more beautiful in his resemblance to Him [Jesus], who bore a face which was viewed with delight by the angels."[4]

These passages, however, do not justify the queer gaze that Kenny repeatedly describes regarding Jogues's admiration of the young Iroquois boys.

In the poem, "Bear," we find the first hints of Jogues's supposed boy lust:

> His eye
> is always either on pelts or dis-
> tracted by the boys.[5]

and

> If he would leave
> the children alone . . . children make men . . .
> I would not interfere with his
> breathing.[6]

This sentiment is repeated in "Wolf Aunt," and again in, a second poem titled, "Bear," with the following lines. Wolf Aunt fears for her adopted son, Jogues's, life: "[fearful] that some boy would resent his stares."[7] Bear reiterates more forcefully, "Yet, stared / at the young boys swimming nude / in the river" then while speaking of the possibility of Wolf Aunt or her daughter nourishing Jogues's lust "(Yet I fear / he abstained, refused that pleasure / while staring at the nude boys playing games.)"[8]

I, personally, find this queering of the voice problematic. By fixing Jogues as a kind of orientalizing pedophile awed by the Natives' "naked, reddish-brown bodies / glisten[ing] like metal in the sunlight."[9] Kenny perpetuates a dangerous stereotype of not only the queer male, but also Catholic priests and brothers specifically. I fear accuracy of the historical gives way to a desire to queer the text in a way that is unfounded and perhaps even detrimental to the normalizing toward which queer writers currently strive.

Giving voice to these people serves to round out history, yet it is the responsibility of the writer to give voice to only that which can be supported, especially when we have the historical figure in question's own words. I think of the contemporary Native fiction writers—how they have learned from their communities and from the oral tradition that it is all the tellings collectively that add up to a more complete reality. Native authors from such disparate tribes as Sherman Alexie (Spokane / Couer d'Alene), Greg Sarris (Pomo / Miwok), Louise Erdrich and David Treuer (Anishnaabe), and Eric Gansworth (Onondaga) employ a style of writing that allows for each chapter to be told from a different character's viewpoint while the stories overlap. In the end, we are left with many views of the same event, and we are invited as readers to participate in coming to a likely reality. This is how Maurice Kenny's *Blackrobe* collection functions. We are reminded that history is often one-sided and recorded by the "winners," if there are any winners in this history.

In giving a voice to Kiosaeton's thoughts on meeting Jogues, we are reminded that there was an Iroquois acceptance or tolerance of others' beliefs, as long as those views were not forced on others. This forcible proselytizing had a much different result. We enter into a dialogue through Kenny's poems, causing us to think out both sides. Kiosaeton speaks to Jogues in the poem bearing his name:

> Eat now. You are in safe
> country with my people
> who will respect your customs
> and invite you into the lodge
> if you maintain respect for ours.[10]

From Jogues's journal, in the poem, "Approaching the Mohawk Village," we learn his thoughts:

> I enter the village
> my silver cross held upright
> though they told me to keep
> it hidden in the folds of my robe.[11]

And later, he remarks on "The People of the Flint:"

> I openly refute their foolish tales / that the world was built on a turtle's back . . .
> And the absurd woman who fell from the sky. . .
> I'll persuade / them to the skirts of Mary, virgin mother / of Christ . . .[12]

This complete disregard for the others' beliefs, coupled with an insistence on forcing his own convictions would lead to Jogues's "crumpling under the club."

The first poem in the epilogue gives voice to Kateri Tekakwitha, the Mohawk girl born in Ossernenoṇ (present day Auriesville, New York) in 1656 to an Algonquin Christian mother and a non-Christian Mohawk father. She was orphaned in 1670, when a smallpox epidemic claimed the lives of her parents, and she was adopted by an aunt and uncle. Kateri was baptized in 1676, and persecuted by non-Christian Mohawks, she fled to Kahnawake, Canada. She died at the age of twenty-four on April 17, 1680, and upon her death her face was healed of smallpox scars. She was declared venerable by Pope Pius XII in 1943 and "Blessed" by Pope John Paul II in 1980. She still awaits canonization.

While Kateri is a culture hero among not only Mohawks but also Catholic Natives across the country, and represents missionary success to the Jesuits, Kenny makes clear in Kateri's monologue ("Tekawitha [Kateri]") the reason why other Mohawks would have persecuted her:

> I shall atone for the sins of my people,
> and for my own sins of ignorance and blasphemy.
> My zeal will obtain penance and my spirit peace.[13]

That Kateri turned so completely to accept her people's theology and belief systems as "ignorance and blasphemy," would indeed be a slap in the face to traditionals. Kenny also recognizes in his poem the previously mentioned erotic ecstasy present in so many historical accounts of religious conversation and self-flagellation. Kateri states:

> Friend, be kind, accept this whip.
> Like winter wind let its leather thongs
> scream through the air and strike my flesh.
> Like the juice of the raspberry blood shall
> trickle from my shoulder blades, my arms.[14]

Here, the physical body is reclaimed, another element of Kenny's poetry that is so very important to me as a writer. Just as history is so often without voice, it also is most often devoid of a body, that one sure thing that we all carry with us. As the voice of Bear speaks in the poem, "Bear," "he [Jogues] could not bear the sight / of naked flesh, nor two people / coupling in the shadows of the lodge."[15] History has never been bodiless—not then, not now. Kenny returns desire to Jogues, as we read of his appreciation for the physical beauty of the Natives: "Naked, reddish-brown bodies / glisten like metal in the sunlight . . ." and "It is exciting to be / here amongst these fetching / people . . . rogues we Jesuits / will change into angels and saints." ("Les Hures").[16]

In the poems written as a record of Kenny's own life, the body is present. In the poem, "Sweat," the body is chronicled as it slips into the bathtub:

> feet and calves,
> thighs and testicles
> dare to slide
> into the depths

of hell.
and
waves of thought
the wave of scalding
water lapping
first the testicles
then nipples
at the edge.[17]

Maurice's writing returns a voice and body to Native poetry, resisting the prescribed notion that all Native poetry should refer to Father Sky, Mother Earth, the buffalo hunt (even for those of us not from the great plains), and eagle. We are human above all, and the body has never been hidden away in Native culture and storytelling. Not only does Maurice Kenny write to inform us of his experience as a contemporary Native, but he offers up voices and emotions to consider from the past. *Consider*—such a beautiful word, coming from the same root as sidereal or star related, to study the stars so carefully you are *con sidere* or *with the stars*.

My own life continued along a similar route to Kenny's, from rural New York State to Brooklyn, then out west, and even to the small village of Fredonia in western New York where Maurice once taught courses in a then just blossoming Women's Studies Program. He was invited to Fredonia after writing the book, *Tekonwatonti*, which gives voice to Mohawk, Molly Brant, who lived during Revolutionary War days. It was not until 2002 that I would meet Maurice Kenny. After moving back to Iroquoia, to teach at the State University of New York (SUNY) Fredonia, I read in the paper that Maurice would be reading at the Native American Community Services Center in Buffalo, New York. I attended the reading with my brother, and Maurice signed my book, "James, So glad to finally take your hand in mine. In friendship, Maurice."

I was fortunate to be able to invite Maurice to SUNY Fredonia for a reading and to share food and stories with him, my mother, and younger brother. I have been to SUNY Potsdam to read and visit with Maurice's class and, again, spend time over more good food and laughter. I am thankful to Maurice for paving the way, for writing about what it means to be Native in the present, not five hundred years ago. I am indebted to him for reminding me also to look to the past—at everything in between that has enabled us to be who we are now—Kanienkehaka. Nia'weh:kowa, Maurice.

NOTES

1. Maurice Kenny, *Carving Hawk: New and Selected Poems, 1953–2000* (Buffalo, NY: White Pine Press, 2002): 190, 8–10.

2. Ibid., 215:6–12.

3. Ibid., 215:15–17.

4. Greer, Allan, ed. *The Jesuit Relations* (New York: Bedford/St. Martin's, 2000): 165.

5. Kenny, *Carving Hawk*, 127:11–13.

6. Ibid., 127:17–20.

7. Ibid., 132:51.

8. Ibid., 136–137:22–24 and 56–58.

9. Ibid., 121:1–2.

10. Ibid., 124:15–19.

11. Ibid., 126:1–4.

12. Ibid., 129:1–2, 8, and 18–20.

13. Ibid., 143:18–20.

14. Ibid., 143:21–25.

15. Ibid., 136:16–18.

16. Ibid., 121:1–2 and 12–15.

17. Ibid., 303:9–13 and 44–49.

FOUR

DANCING BACK STRONG OUR NATIONS

Performance as Continuance in Maurice Kenny's Poetry

Qwo-Li Driskill

Maurice Kenny is an elder to me as a Native, Queer, Two-Spirit, mixed-blood poet. I first read Kenny's work in the 1988 collection *Gay and Lesbian Poetry in Our Time* edited by Joan Larkin and Carl Morse.[1] In the early and mid-1990s I was living in a small university town in conservative Colorado, and this collection was a lifeline to me in many ways, not the least was the inclusion of a handful of Native writers including Beth Brant, Chrystos, the late Vickie Sears, and Kenny. Kenny's poem "Winkte" helped give me hope and strength that regardless of the kinds of homophobic attacks that I faced on almost a daily basis, that many Native traditions hold precedents for people who fall outside of white supremacist gender and sexual roles. Kenny, and other Two-Spirit writers, helped me remember that "We had power with the people."[2] So it is with honor and respect for what poetry does, and for what Kenny has done for us as Native people—particularly Two-Spirit people—that this essay emerges.[3]

In her introduction to Maurice Kenny's *Dancing Back Strong the Nation*, Paula Gunn Allen writes that Kenny's poetry reminds us "that it is quite possible for each of us to join in Dancing Back Strong the Nation."[4] Kenny's poetry does important rhetorical, theoretical, and political work. His poetry argues for Native people to engage with our lifeways as a means not only to resist colonialism, but also to ensure the continuance of our communities and traditions. I am particularly interested in Kenny's use of traditional performance in his poetry because of my commitment to relearning my own performance traditions and lifeways and because, as Performance Studies scholar Diana Taylor argues, "By taking performance seriously as a system of learning, storing, and transmitting knowledge, performance studies allows us to expand what we understand by 'knowledge.' This move, for starters, might prepare us to challenge the preponderance of writing in Western epistemologies."[5] Taylor's work and Michel de Certeau's notion of *practice* are both useful here in my analysis, as they encourage an examination of the importance of what bodies *do*. de Certeau's theory of practice provides an understanding the ways in which performance can be used to subvert power structures:

> Dwelling, moving about, speaking, reading, shopping, and cooking are activities that seem to correspond to the characteristics of tactical ruses and surprises: clever tricks of the "weak" within the established order of the "strong," and art of putting one over on the adversary on his own turf, hunter's tricks, maneuverable, polymorph mobilities, jubilant, poetic, and warlike discoveries.[6]

Performance as a means to interpret Native literatures aids us in disrupting oral / literate binaries that simplify and erase the complexities of Native peoples' rhetorical / artistic traditions and elucidate the ways in which performance as a *practice* disrupts colonial projects.[7]

Dance is a central mechanism for cultural maintenance in many of our communities. Cherokee scholar Charlotte Heth writes, "Indian music and dance pervade all aspects of life, from creation stories to death and remembrance of death. The importance of American Indian dance is found in both in its impact on modern society and in the traditions and values it expresses to and for the Indian peoples."[8] As is the case with many Native performance traditions, Mohawk performance traditions help to maintain community relationships, identities, memories, and responsibilities. By using performance as a rhetorical device in his poetry, Kenny compels Native people to dance (back) strong nations injured through colonial violence, restoring and continuing community memory and identity.

PERFORMANCE AS CONTINUANCE

The concept of continuance has been a major concern for Native people throughout our histories, particularly since the invasion and colonization of our homelands. Continuance as a central poetic theme of Native women was placed at the center of Paula Gunn Allen's essay "Answering the Deer: Genocide and Continuance in the Poetry of American Indian Women" in *The Sacred Hoop: Recovering the Feminine in American Indian Traditions*.[9] I think that Allen's preface to that book holds a clear articulation of what *continuance* means and entails for Native people:

> [I]t is of the utmost importance to our continuing recovery that we recognize our astonishing survival against all odds; that we congratulate ourselves . . . for our amazing ability to endure, recover, restore our ancient values and life ways, and then blossom. . . . There is surely cause to weep, to grieve; but greater than ugliness, the endurance of tribal beauty is our reason to sing, to greet the coming day and the restored life and hope it brings.[10]

The conclusion of Robert Warrior's *Tribal Secrets* likewise expresses the need for continuance: "Our struggle at the moment is to continue to survive and work toward a time when we can replace the need for being preoccupied with survival with a more responsible and peaceful way of living within communities and with the ever-changing landscape that will ever be our only home."[11] Continuance celebrates our survival and ensures the future of our communities.

Continuance is the survival of cultural memories and practices as a mode of resistance to settler-colonialism. Taylor takes the position that "performance transmits memories, makes political claims, and manifests a group's sense of identity."[12] Performance—including powwow, ceremonial dance, contemporary theater, song, and storytelling—is central to the continuance of our traditions and nations. W. Richard West, Jr. (Southern Cheyenne) affirms this idea:

> Dance is the very embodiment of Indigenous values and represents the response of Native Americans to complex and sometimes difficult historical experiences. Music and dance combine with material culture, language, spirituality, and artistic expression in compelling and complex ways, and are definitive elements of native identity. Dance reflects the vast capacity of native peoples to endure culturally and to continue as a vital cotemporary cultural phenomenon, notwithstanding historical oppression and a way of being that stands in stark contrast, if not rebuttal, to much that drives the current technological age. The dance of native peoples is thus both a vital means of surviving culturally and a powerful expression of that survival.[13]

Much of Kenny's poetry is concerned with continuance, and this often is demonstrated through his attention to performance, particularly dance traditions. Kenny is such a prolific writer that it isn't possible within one essay to examine all of the ways in which he uses performance in his poetry to the extent that I would like, so I will focus on *Dancing Back Strong the Nation* as well as the poems "The Hands of Annie-Mae" and "New Song" because they exemplify relationships between performance and continuance in Kenny's work.[14]

Themes of resistance and continuance through performance are central to much of Kenny's poetry. Nowhere is this more evident than in his 1979 collection *Dancing Back Strong the Nation*. In the poem "I Went North," Kenny makes the central argument of the collection, that it is through participation with our traditional lifeways that Native people can help ensure our continuance:

> I went north in winter
> they were dancing in the Longhouse
> women danced
> old men danced
> children danced
> We ate cornbread.[15]

The poem roots itself firmly within Haudenosaunee Longhouse traditions, creating a picture of a community that sustains itself through dancing. Linley B. Logan (Seneca) discusses the importance of Longhouse dance traditions to Haudenosaunee continuance:

> The future of the Confederacy's social, political, and religious existence for the "seventh generation.: . . . depends on nurturing the children of today. . . . The present generation of Native American youth is the seed to an integral cycle of cultural renewal and growth. In increasing numbers, young Iroquois women and men are embracing the responsibility to learn, and participate in, their ceremonies and dances.[16]

"I Went North," like Haudenosaunee dance traditions, continues by acknowledging humans as part of a community and the more-than-human world: "I . . . / heard wolf / heard a child cry / heard the drum."[17] Relationships among humans, the larger universe, and ceremonial performance meet in the Longhouse of Kenny's poem. And, it is through performance that the Haudenosaunee continue: "I knew they would dance back strong the Nation."[18]

Because in many of Kenny's poems "north" is the direction of the Mohawk Nation, the dancing in the Longhouse is also part of the speaker's return home to Mohawk traditions and landbases. Poems such as this are a tool to heal from manifestations of colonialism in which many Native people are estranged from their communities and traditions. In "Going Home," the voice of the poem mourns this disconnection from Mohawk performance traditions: "home from Brooklyn to the reservation / that was not home / to songs I could not sing / to dances I could not dance."[19] The images of the Longhouse community "dancing back strong the Nation," then, help return the speaker to a continuing tradition.

Poems interspersed throughout *Dancing Back Strong the Nation* create a drum-and-rattle rhythm that pulls the reader through the collection, mirroring the call and response pattern of Haudenosaunee stomp dance traditions. The poems "Drums," "Dance," and "Moccasin" ask the reader to "listen" to songs and dances in order to ensure community continuance. "Drums" begins:

> listen . . .
> drums drum
>   dance dance
> rattles rattle
>   sing sing

And concludes "listen . . . / thunder thunder / shakes / thunder shakes the floor."[20] A call to "listen" also opens the poems "Dance" and "Moccasin."[21] Asking readers to "listen" is a call for them to pay close attention to the importance of dance to community survival, to embody the reciprocal relationships among people and between people and the world around them, and to respond to the call through community participation. Ron LaFrance (Mohawk) explains that in Haudenosaunee social dance traditions that the speaker at the dance event "will announce, 'People, listen, we are again lucky, the singers are in abundance and are ready to sing for the enjoyment this evening.' Then he will introduce the dance, the name or names of the singers and the leaders, and invite all to participate."[22] The voice in the dance-specific poems in *Dancing Back Strong the Nation* functions similarly as the speaker in Haudenosaunee social dance, calling the people to participate in community and reminding them why they are present. In "Dance" Kenny writes, "We come to greet and thank / the strawberry plants . . . mice in the grass / chicory in the fields / owl on a branch / . . . We come to greet and thank / We come / to dance."[23]

Dancing Back Strong the Nation has at its heart images of renewal and thanksgiving and healing from the devastation of colonialism through using Mohawk dance images and rhythms as poetic devices that make a specific rhetorical claim: Through engagement with our communities' performance traditions, Native people and nations continue.

Dance takes a central place in a very different poem, "The Hands of Annie-Mae Aquash." This poem disturbs the reader through the use of violent and dismembered imagery that reminds us of the brutality of

Pictou-Aquash's murder and the dismemberment of Pictou-Aquash's body after her murder. Kenny's poem here grapples with the continuing violence against Native people in general and Native women specifically and also argues for performance and ceremony as an antidote to this kind of violence.

The two opening sections of the poem, "I. 1976" and "II. 1989" evoke the horror of Annie Mae's death and connects her murder and dismemberment to a history of dominant Christian European / Euro-American patriarchal violence. These sections remind us that her murder, far from an isolated incident, is woven into a history of colonialism on this continent and elsewhere. In "I. 1976," the poem argues that it is the mercenaries of this power structure, "masters of medieval torture who school the world in / depravity" that "strive to keep breath / in Salem and the ax hot from human pain" that are responsible for the crime.[24] This section's reference to Salem, and earlier references to medieval torture, reminds the reader of the violence that has emerged from Christian vehemence and patriarchal violence. In "II. 1989," Kenny continues to look at the relationships between other instances of violence, colonialism, and genocide with Pictou-Aquash's assassination: "Students, heads bowed in shame / in the horror, too startled by your murder to protest. They have seen Sand Creek, My Lai / and now the massacre of you. . . ."[25]

Juxtaposed with images of colonial and patriarchal violence are references to dance and ceremony that shift the poem from a place of defeat and fear to acts of witness, continuance, and action. Section "III" of the poem asks the audience to remember the goals of Pictou-Aquash's decolonial activism. The tenderness of this section is almost jarring after the violence of the earlier stanzas and with the knowledge of Pictou-Aquash's murder firmly within the psyches of most of Kenny's readers. Images of Native performances and spiritualities are used rhetorically here to make a very specific argument regarding Native people's responsibility in struggles for continuance and resistance:

> All you ever wanted was milk in your breasts
> for the children; corn and rabbit
> for the generations; cleanliness
> for the earth for naked feet to touch
> while dancing on the belly of their mother;
> freedom from want . . . is that so much to ask;
> respect for a grave, respect for a prayer,
> respect for the first moon and the first sun
> rising slowly over turtle's back.
> Rage is not sufficient.[26]

Cultural continuance is clearly articulated through images of the cycles of death and renewal. Images of milk, children, past and future generations are joined together with respect for the dead, prayer, and the universe through the lines "cleanliness / for the earth for naked feet to touch / while dancing on the belly of their mother."[27] The image "dancing on the belly of their mother" is the visual central line of the stanza, creating a link between desires for continuance expressed in the beginning and the means to attain continuance through engaged respect and reciprocity with the world around us outlined in the end of the stanza before the section's closing argument, "Rage is not sufficient."[28] Dance, and by extension other embodied cultural traditions, becomes the vehicle with which we can join the need for continuance with the need for respectful interactions with our communities and the larger world around us.

Although Part III of this poem directly addresses Pictou-Aquash, as do the II and IV sections, this section also specifically addresses a Native readership. These desires were and are the driving force behind Pictou-Aquash's passionate activism and many Native activists. Kenny's specific reference to dance here reminds his readers of the reciprocal relationship between dance and community responsibility. "Rage is not sufficient" as a reaction to the specific atrocities surrounding Annie Mae Pictou-Aquash, nor as a means for cultural continuance. Instead, the poem suggests, we must react to colonial violence through engaged and embodied action and intentional engagement with our traditions. The repetition of the word "respect" reminds us of what is necessary if we are to hope for a future.

Dance is again used in the last section of the poem, which braids together the themes, images, and concerns introduced in the earlier sections. Pictou-Aquash's murdered and dismembered body is reclaimed in hopes that continued resistance can emerge in the wake of such heinous crimes. Kenny complexly brings together images of dismemberment and murder with continuance and hope:

> I kiss those severed fingers one by one
> hoping to suck out your courage
> and defiance, your strength as seed
> to replant, harvest, to nourish
> the very young of the people, all people.
> Finger by fingertip I kiss the flesh
> and suck your blood which spurts
> from your life . . . as long as drums bang
> and songs remain the essence of human-kind.
> I lay the eagle prayer feather

on your figurative grave,
knowing well, rage is not enough
nor revenge satisfactory.[29]

The disturbing and almost vampiristic images in this section remind readers of their responsibility to remember the legacy of Pictou-Aquash and everyone's culpability in systems of violence and oppression. Our struggles are able to continue only because of those who have fought and suffered before us. We literally fight and survive on lands holding our ancestors' blood. Yet, it is through the constant reclaiming of our ancestors' bodies and histories—however brutal—that we are able to continue as Native people and as human beings. Pictou-Aquash's memory and resistance is kept alive through our practices: "as long as drums bang / and songs remain the essence of human-kind."

The last poem I examine is the exquisite piece "New Song" originally printed in *In the Time of the Present.*

NEW SONG

We are turning
  eagles wheeling sky
We are rounding
  sun moving in the air
We are listening
  to old stories
Our spirits to the breeze
  the voices are speaking
Our hearts touch earth
  and feel dance in our feet
Our minds in clear thought
  we speak the old words
We will remember everything
  knowing who we are
We will touch our children
  and they will dance and sing
As eagle turns, sun rises, winds blow,
  ancestors be our guides
Into new bloodless tomorrows.[30]

This "new song" is about continuance and imagining futures for our communities free from genocide and violence. The poem is not only about survival, but also renewal. The poem's heartbeat rhythm accompanies us as Native readers through the images of dance that are the center of the poem. It is through dance that healing takes place and continuance becomes possible: "We will remember everything / knowing who we are / We will touch our children / and they will dance and sing." And it is through dance that our relationships with the more-than-human world and our ancestors is affirmed and our futures made possible: "As eagle turns, sun rises, winds blow, / ancestors be our guides / Into new bloodless tomorrows." Kenny does not locate "tradition" within a mythic past, but conceives it as a present practice and imagined future, one in which new songs emerge out of the old.

RAGE IS NOT SUFFICIENT

Like most Indians in academia, my investment in scholarship comes from its possibilities to aid in larger struggles for social justice. During some of the more bizarre, arcane, or disheartening moments within the Ivory Tower, I carry Indiana Miami / Eastern Shawnee scholar-activist Malea Powell's challenge and reminder with me: "That is, after all, why we do this scholarly thing we do—isn't it? To change the world? To learn how to solve contemporary problems in productive and generous ways?"[31] And, perhaps also like many Indians in academia, I believe that scholarship should not be separated from movements and communities outside of the academy, and that there needs to be continued activism inside and outside of academic circles to ensure that our work is useful to movements for decolonization. Maurice Kenny's work is vital for its implications for artists, activists, and scholars in practice.

As Native artists, we have a specific obligation to aid in the struggles of our communities through our art. At the forefront of our struggles are finding ways to engage responsibly with decolonization, sovereignty, healing, and continuance. Kenny's work, both examined in this essay and more broadly, offers us a model from which to create art that aids in continuance.

Although Kenny uses numerous poetic structures and forms in his work from countless poetic traditions and influences, his use of dance rhythms as the meter of some of the poems opens up interesting poetic possibilities for Native writers. Much has been said about Native poetry being rooted in ceremonial chanting, traditional song, and other oral traditions. As a poet, I get excited about the possibilities of also examining and creating poetry that uses traditional dance and rhythms as metric and tonal structures. Kenny's poems in *Dance Back Strong the Nation* engage these traditional strategies, and this practice offers another source to create, and continue Native formal poetry. Kenny's poetry allows me to imagine poetry that, for instance, follows the rhythmic structures and tonalities of shell shaking and Cherokee stomp dance songs.

Native poetry *is* activism. Native poets are very aware of this, and it is my hope that other Native activists continue to engage with poetry and other arts as powerful tools for social justice. Native poetry also provides critiques and theories for Native activist movements. Part of what we have to learn as activists in Native communities is the centrality of our traditions to activist struggles. Kenny's poetry reminds Native activists that part of the core work that must be done is active and intentional engagement with our lifeways. Our languages, our songs, our dances, and our arts are central to our resistance. They require active engagement in order to continue.

As important as organizations such as the American Indian Movement (AIM) have been to Native struggles, like many nationalist struggles they have tended to disregard feminist and Queer / Two-Spirit concerns, among others, often furthering colonial mindsets in the process. "The Hands of Annie-Mae" is rife with implications for activists. Although this poem was published before trials that revealed AIM's responsibility for Pictou-Aquash's murder, it contains a particularly poignant and haunting warning to Native activists. Echoing earlier arguments, the closing phrase of the poem, "rage is not enough / nor revenge satisfactory" opens layered meanings when interpreted with an understanding of AIM's involvement with the murder. Rage and revenge are insufficient to respond; moreover, they are insufficient tools for activism that, left unchecked or engaged with uncritically, can lead to brutality. Because Pictou-Aquash's murder took place within a context of patriarchal organizing, and her story has become a symbol for both the resistance of and violence against Native women, Kenny's closing phrase here becomes a specific warning to male-dominated nationalist movements.

There are numerous implications for academics in engaging with Kenny's work, not the least of which is the importance of teaching Kenny within our classes. Furthermore, Kenny's work reminds us of the centrality of bodies within our work as scholars because Kenny argues for embodied *practice* rather than distanced and unengaged intellectualism. Robert Warrior looks to poetry as a model for resistance and scholarship:

> In developing American Indian critical studies, we need to practice the same sort of intellectual sovereignty that many Native poets practice. As many of the poets find their work continuous with, but not circumscribed by, Native traditions of storytelling or ceremonial chanting, we can find the work of criticism continuous with Native traditions of deliberation and decision making.[32]

Kenny's call for Native people to dance strong our nations remains an utmost concern for us. I think that we are currently experiencing enormous healing in our communities, even as we continue to face daunting challenges. Our traditions provide the center from which to engage these challenges and are themselves acts of resistance that ensure our continuance. Through them, "We will remember everything."

NOTES

1. Joan Larkin and Carl Morse. Eds. *Gay and Lesbian Poetry in Our Time: An Anthology* (New York: St. Martins, 1988).

2. Maurice Kenny, *Carving Hawk: New and Selected Poems* (Buffalo: White Pine, 2002), 84:31.

3. Although this is not an explicitly Queer or Two-Spirit analysis of Kenny's poetry, both the contexts and concerns of this essay *are* Two-Spirit. Not only is this an analysis of a Two-Spirit writer by another Two-Spirit writer, I think that current Two-Spirit movements have a particular concern with the reclaiming and continuing embodied practices that place us within historical and cultural contexts. Two-Spirit movements are themselves models for what "continuance" means. Furthermore, I think that it is necessary to remember how many Two-Spirit people have helped, and continue to help, build Native scholarly, artistic, and activist communities.

4. Kenny, *Dancing Back Strong the Nation: Poems* (Buffalo, NY: White Pine, 1981), 2.

5. Diana Taylor, *The Archive and the Repertoire: Performing Cultural Memory in the Americas* (Durham, NC: Duke University, 2003), 16.

6. Michel de Certeau, *The Practice of Everyday Life* (Berkeley: University of California, 2002), 40.

7. Taylor argues that "The rift . . . does not lie between the written and spoken word, but between the *archive* of supposedly enduring materials (i.e., texts, documents, buildings, bones) and the so-called ephemeral *repertoire* of embodied practice/knowledge (i.e., spoken language, dance, sports, ritual." Taylor, *The Archive and the Repertoire*, 19.

8. Charlotte Heth, ed, *Native American Dance: Ceremonies and Social Traditions* (Washington, DC: National Museum of the American Indian Smithsonian Institution, 1992), 17.

9. Paula Gunn Allen, *The Sacred Hoop: Recovering the Feminine in American Indian Traditions* (Boston: Beacon, 1992), 155–164.

10. Ibid., xi.

11. Robert Allen Warrior, *Tribal Secrets: Recovering American Indian Intellectual Tradition* (Minneapolis: University of Minnesota, 1995), 126.

12. Taylor, *The Archive and the Repertoire*, xvii.

13. Heth, *Native American Dance*, ix.

14. Although I am focusing on dance traditions for this chapter, I think that Kenny's historical poems can also seen as linked intimately to the recitation of wampum records. Kenny's *Blackrobe* and *Tekonwatonti: Molly Brant*, in particular, both document and imagine Mohawk history and, like wampum recitations, use the performative to transmit memory and history. Angela Hass' (Eastern Cherokee) scholarship on wampum records reminds us of their significance as an embodied and performed rhetoric:

> Wampum records are maintained by regularly revisiting and re-"reading" them through community memory and performance, as wampum is a living rhetoric that communicates a mutual relationship between two or more

> parties, despite the lack of one of those parties to live up to that promise (which we know was the result of most wampum treaties with the colonists). Thus, wampum embodies memory, as it extends human memories of inherited knowledges through interconnected, non-linear designs with associative message storage and retrieval methods.

Angela M. Haas, "Wampum as Hypertext: An American Indian Intellectual Tradition of Multimedia Theory and Practice," *Studies in American Indian Literatures* 19, no. 4 (2007): 80–81.

15. Kenny, *Dancing Back*, 62:6.

16. Heth, *Native American Dance*, 27.

17. Kenny, *Dancing Back*, 62:7–10.

18. Ibid., 62:11.

19. Kenny, *Carving Hawk: New and Selected Poems* (Buffalo, NY: White Pine Press, 2002), 68:12.

20. Ibid., 63:14–17.

21. Ibid., 65:1, 66:1.

22. Heth, *Native American Dance*, 23.

23. Kenny, *Dancing Back*, 65:13–14 and 21–23.

24. Kenny, *Carving Hawk*, 296:8–12.

25. Ibid., 297:25–28.

26. Ibid., 297:33–42.

27. Ibid., 297:35–37.

28. Ibid., 297:42.

29. Ibid., 297–298:43–55.

30. Ibid., 285:17–19.

31. Malea D. Powell, "Down by the River, or How Susan La Flesche Picotte Can Teach us about Alliance as a Practice of Survivance," *College English* 67 no. 1. (2004): 57.

32. Warrior, *Tribal Secrets*, 118.

FIVE

MAURICE KENNY

How Can Any Self-Respecting Mohawk Live in a Place Like Brooklyn?

Susan Ward

I.

Maurice Kenny was born in rural upstate New York, in that section between the Black and the St. Lawrence rivers called the North Country. He grew up near Watertown, New York, on Lake Ontario within sight of the Adirondack mountains. But his life's journey has taken him many places—to the Midwest, back to Watertown, to New York City, to Mexico, to Puerto Rico and the U.S. Virgin Islands, to Chicago, back to New York City, and, finally back home. Of all these places, the North Country and New York City are most important to Kenny and his poetry. Opposite environments, they represent opposites in Kenny's life and work—country versus city, nature versus the man-made, Native versus non-Native concerns, themes, and forms. His movement between them follows a pattern traced by many Native American writers who journeyed from often rural homelands to urban areas or centers of academic learning and then back home to write from and about their native roots. It also recalls the theme critic William Bevis has called "homing," a theme which traces the same pattern in the plots of many American novels.[1]

This chapter explores the physical journey from home to city to home again in the life and works of Maurice Kenny. It also explores the way in which the city furnished Kenny with important thematic material, making him one of the few Native American writers to look to the city as well as to his rural home for inspiration for his work.

To begin, we must turn to some of Kenny's to autobiographical statements in recorded or published interviews. Born of a Mohawk father and a mother of Seneca lineage, Kenny says, that, as a child, he was not overly conscious of his Native heritage.[2] What he was conscious of was the natural beauty around him. He wrote:

> Surely, because my father found so much beauty and joy in the woods and the lakes and rivers, I too found this same beauty and freedom. I learned, walking these meadows edging the woods, crossed by the various streams, that I could make up songs not merely of my loneness but of the loneness and the beauty of these other creatures.[3]

At the same time, he developed a voracious appetite for books. He credits an elderly neighbor with giving him "respect for the written word" and recalls visits to bookstores in Watertown where, backed by his father's charge accounts, he purchased anthologies containing all kinds of literature.[4] He studied for a degree at Butler University, and, later, took courses at St. Lawrence University. He read Blake, Donne, Keats, Whitman, Robinson Jeffers, Louise Bogan, Robert Frost, and the plays of Eugene O'Neil and Shakespeare. Eventually, in 1957, he took a Greyhound bus to New York City, which became his home base for the next 25 years.

In New York, Kenny found a job at the 59th Street Marboro bookstore and was immediately surrounded by what he has called "the artistic pulse of the city."[5] He rubbed elbows with actors, writers, and editors. He taught history of drama at Mary Tarcai's School of Drama. He studied poetry writing with Louise Bogan at New York University.[6] Under her influence, he published *Dead Letters Sent* and two other collections, *With Love to Lesbia* and *And Grieve, Lesbia* both, by his own account, highly imitative of Catullus.[7] His first decade in New York was a time of tremendous artistic excitement, important for his contact with Bogan and as the time of his first major publications, but his work during this period did not deal with Native materials.

Kenny credits the occupation of Alcatraz in 1969, his reading of Mari Sandoz's *Cheyenne Autumn* around 1970, and the confrontations at Wounded Knee in 1973–1974 with bringing him "home" to Native themes. "It was time as a poet to forget John Crowe Ransom, Eliot, Frost, yes, even William Carlos Williams, Jeffers, and Miss Bogan herself, and become myself," he writes in "Introduction: A Memoir." At the same time, Louise Bogan was encouraging him to write about his Native heritage. In 1974, he journeyed north to Akwesasne, and began to work with those producing the journal *Akwesasne Notes*. "I started researching myself," he said in an interview in 2002. "Where else would you research [your Mohawk] self except Akwesasne?"[8] He began going up to the Akwesasne Reservation in northern New York weekends and summers. In 1973, his poem "I Am the Sun," based on a Lakota-Sioux Ghost Dance song, was published in *Akwesasne Notes*. The collection *North: Poems of Home* (Blue Cloud Quarterly Press) was published in 1977, and another, *Dancing Back Strong the Nation* (White Pine Press), in 1979. Maurice Kenny's career as a poet whose work was grounded firmly in Native themes and traditions had begun.

Yet he continued to live in New York City. New York City in the 1970s and early 1980s provided Kenny with the locus for two important literary ventures: his co-editing of the literary review *Contact II* with J. G. Gosiak and his founding and directing of Strawberry Press. His work with *Contact II* put him in contact with some of the most progressive new poets of the day. The roster of Native American poets he published through Strawberry Press includes some of the best-known Native writers of the twentieth century: Paula Gunn Allen, Peter Blue Cloud, Joy Harjo, Lance Henson, and Wendy Rose, to name only a few. Remaining in the city thus helped to foster Kenny's growth as a poet and as a Native writer in ways that complemented his experiences at Akwesasne.

II.

The city appears as an important image in a number of Kenny's poems written in the 1970s and 1980s. In the poem "On Second Thought," Kenny admits to liking the city for its literary associations. "I've never wanted to live in Brooklyn," he writes, "but I've been enjoying the ghosts / of Crane, Wolfe and Mailer."[9] Autumn City," which Kenny claims is one of his few poems to deal with the city in a contemporary context, provides an example of his ability to depict the city in imagistic terms:

"Autumn City"

Vlaminck skies
            flaunt, ruffle sunset
over Hudson
        harbor and ships
up the twin towers
            hard fire climbing
window
        upon window
molten clouds

disintegrate
over black-
ening streets
spires
impale stars
cat-eyes
sprinkle the rivers
parks
linger in fear
as pearls
burst
against
the jet throats
of bridges and
highways which cover
Seyseys'grave.[10]

The poems that make up *Last Mornings in Brooklyn* continue this technique. In the opening poem, Kenny pays homage to William Carlos Williams: "7 a.m. / I put down Williams' *Paterson* / and pick up the street . . . / a strange landscape"; the remaining 45 vignettes picture scenes viewed from Kenny's window—a busboy going to work, a Korean greengrocer emptying a bucket, and so on.[11] In these works, the treatment of the city as subject is largely positive.

The everyday horrors of the city, however, particularly its violence, also surface in Kenny's poetry of this period. Perhaps no poem embodies this theme more vividly than "Summer Night Incident on Atlantic Ave., Brooklyn," in which he writes of the death by a hit-and-run driver of an old Mexican man. Kenny notes elsewhere that this incident was "another one of those experiences in which I went into a towering rage."[12] The poem "Last Night . . . ," in which the narrator's landlady advises "this morning . . . / . . .nobody's been / murdered / here, but / this is Brooklyn," continues this theme.[13]

As Kenny began to fashion his own poetry around Native American themes, however, the city began to function as a symbol of all that is antithetical to a Native way of life. In "Autumn City," the last two lines remind the reader of the Carnarsee chief, Seyse, who sold Manhattan Island to the Dutch. In "Young Male," the narrator, observing a young white man sitting across the aisle in a subway car, reminds the reader / listener that every white can be associated in some way with the European invaders who destroyed Native lands and traditions: "Your face is not ugly / nor does it appear particularly mean," he muses, "[but] I know you are here to stay /

and that you are scouting buffalo."[14] A consciousness of the division between white and Native America, brought on by confrontation after confrontation in the city, begins to become clear.

In a poem published in the late 1970s, Kenny depicts the story of "Gowane," a young brave who keeps watch for the Canarsee against the "bleached-ones" who have just taken the tip of the island of Minna-atn. The young man keeps his watch successfully, and is therefore given the name "Gowane," "one of little sleep," because "He had stood watch at the watchful place, Gowanus."[15] In this poem, tied to New York City place names, Kenny anticipates a practice he was to bring to fruition in his later poetry, the researching and reimagining of sometimes-obscure pieces of Native American history.

As his thoughts turned to his ancestral and cultural home in the north, the city also began to function as a place of longing for Kenny. In "Wine Grapes," a cluster of grapes offered by a friend in the city transports the speaker in thought to his other home. He writes: "sitting in Brooklyn in the shadow of the bridge / sharp light, cold and clear, spreads / across cement and sky; fingers quiver to pick / as they did last summer sour cherry and black-cap."[16] In "Wild Strawberry," Mexican strawberries, which form their own kind of political statement, remind the speaker of childhood springtimes when he picked strawberries in northern New York. In these poems, the city becomes less attractive as an image, as the poet is pulled more strongly toward the landscape and culture of his northern origin.[17]

The poems in *Last Mornings in Brooklyn*, published in chapbook form in 1991, are Kenny's farewell to the city. The scenes he depicts—the park, the shops, the prostitutes, the newsstands—are all ones he saw or could have seen from his Brooklyn apartment window while waiting for the moving truck to transport him and his belongings back to the Adirondacks. The farewell is not a bitter one. In the epigraph to the collection, he calls Brooklyn "home of so many good / friends I do not leave be- / hind but continue to / carry along—."[18] In the last poem in this volume, he quotes and answers Cheyenne poet Lance Henson's question: "How / can any / self-respecting / Mohawk / live / in a place like this? Response: / I burn / Cedar and Sage / and keep / an eye / on the bridge." The implication is clear: the city is an acceptable place for Native Americans so long as they do not forget their cultural and geographic origins.

In the poem "Writing A Love Letter I Know You will Never Receive," Kenny writes: "They forget / Pueblos were the first apartment dwellers, / that Mohawks built most of these skyscrapers / threatening heads; they forget we always lived / in villages from where we could take / an easy stroll to the cornfields or blackberry patch."[19] Kenny's movement back and forth between Brooklyn and the North Country in the 1970s and 1980s is reminiscent of these lines. Although he left the city to take up permanent residence in the North Country in 1987, the city was never completely alien to him.

III.

It is important to remember that while Kenny was writing the city poems in the 1970s and 1980s, he also was journeying back and forth to Akwesasne and experimenting with the Native themes and forms. As noted previously, his first important work in this vein was "I am the Sun," published in *Akwesasne Notes* in 1973. The poems associated with his "homecoming" to northern New York, also show Kenny returning to his interest in writing about nature, a subject he has acknowledged is at the heart of much of his poetry.[20] In a 1980 essay, critic James Ruppert wrote that Kenny "at times becomes the nature he expresses" and achieves "a fusion with the natural . . . so complete that it is almost unnoticed."[21] But Kenny's poetry from 1973 onward began to move in new directions, as he fused his interest in nature with his interest in Native themes.

The first way in which Kenny's post-1973 nature poetry differs from his earlier work in this genre is in the way he explores the theme of the American landscape corrupted by outside invaders. This becomes a central concern in the collection *North: Poems of Home*, published by Blue Cloud Quarterly in 1977. "Land," from this volume, is a case in point. This excerpt, from the opening section, embodies both the speaker's love of the land and his sorrow for its despoliation:

> Torn, tattered, yet rugged
> in the quick incline of bouldered hills,
> crabappled, cragged, lighting-struck birch, cedar;
> wilderness muzzled; forest . . . kitchen tables and bedposts
> of foreign centuries; meadows cowed
> beyond redemption, endurance, violated
> by emigres feet, and vineyards alien
> to Indigenous squash and berry,
> fragile lupine and iris of the pond;
> even the rivers struggle to the sea
> while wounded willows bend in the snow
> blown north by the west wind.[22]

The poem goes on to juxtapose images of the land unspoiled with reminders of the presence of European invaders in various ages. It ends with the startlingly unpleasant images of "gooseberry . . . diseased, and the elm, / stone walls broken, sky cracked, pheasants / and young muskrats sterilized, and fields."[23] Kenny was to return to this theme often in his later nature poetry.

In his North Country poetry written after 1975, Kenny also began to explore the theme of homecoming, with all the problems that a Native person of mixed-blood origin might encounter. The poems "North: In Memory of My Father," and "Going Home," about the speaker's ride from his city home in Brooklyn to a "home" reservation in New York State, function in this manner. In the latter, he calls Akwesasne the "reservation that was not home" and writes of the confusion of meeting "faces I did not know / and hands which did not recognize me," alluding to a theme found in the works of Native writers from Gertrude Bonnin (Zitkala-a) to James Welch.[24] In the poems written after 1975, Kenny also began to voice an overtly political stance on issues touching Native Americans. "I Am the Sun" provides a good example. Of the composition of this poem, Kenny has written:

> At the time I wrote "I Am The Sun," which was the time of the Wounded Knee confrontation in 1973, I personally was so angry and I physically couldn't do anything about it because I was suffering a heart attack. . . . I couldn't get out and do anything, so I had to sing it out of me. . . . I couldn't use an Iroquois traditional form because I was writing about Lakota people. So I chose a Ghost Dance song.[25]

The poem's form, based as it is on a Lakota-Sioux ghost dance, immediately raises the theme of Native rebellion. Its content centers around this theme.

In the poems from this period onward, Kenny also consciously began to use Native oral traditions and Native rhythms as the basis for his poetry. "I Am the Sun," "Moccasin," and "Drums" all function in this manner. In both "Moccasin" and "Drums," for example, the rhythm is influenced heavily by the rhythm of traditional native dance. And "I Am the Sun," as already noted, is organized in the form of a Sun Dance chant and includes phrases in the original language.

Finally, the imaginative reworking of Native American legend and Native American history became a prominent interest for Kenny. The poem "Akwesasne," dealing with the legends and legacies of Deganawidah and Hiawatha (*North: Poems of Home*), is an early example of his work in this vein. Two later books, *Black Robe*, about Isaac Jogues, and *Tekonwatonti: Molly Brant*, about the sister of Joseph Brant who married Sir William Johnson and after his death became the leader of his British-allied Indian troops during the American Revolution, are important later examples. Kenny himself views these latter two as representing some of his most important work.

There is no doubt that after Kenny returned in spirit and then in body to northern New York, his poetry took a different turn. In his autobiographical essay "Waiting at the Edge," he noted: "All the elements important to my poems, to my life surround me [in the North Country]." And of the connection between his himself and his homeland he has written:

> Northwest of the mountains were my natural water / earth, although I felt attachment to the hills and woods, lands I lived away from for many years. I've come home before it is too late to see the herons, cranes, mallards and kingfisher, hear the cry or song of the loon not as a visitor but as someone who has a natural identity, a natural need to be a part of the north. It was my people, my Sky Woman, whom loon helped to descend safely onto turtle's back.[26]

Native American literature is the richer for Kenny's association with both New York City and with his homeland in the North Country. His movement between these two locales both followed a pattern embodied in the lives of other Native writers and helped to inform his own work.

NOTES

1. William Bevis, "Native American Novels: Homing In," in *Recovering the Word: Essays on Native American Literature*, eds. Brian Swann and Arnold Krupat (Berkeley: University of California Press, 1987), 580.

2. Maurice Kenny, Interview by Susan Ward, 28 October 2002, Potsdam, NY.

3. Maurice Kenny, "Waiting at the Edge," in *I Tell You Now: Autobiographical Essays by Native American Writers*, eds., Brian Swann and Arnold Krupat (Lincoln and London: University of Nebraska Press, 1987), 43.

4. Ibid., 41; idem, Interview, 28 October 2002.

5. Maurice Kenny, "Introduction: A Memoir," in *On Second Thought: A Compilation* (Norman and London: University of Oklahoma Press, 1995), 26.

6. For two accounts by Kenny of Louise Bogan's influence, see "Prelude" to *Between Two Rivers: Selected Poems 1965–1984* (Fredonia, NY: White Pine Press, 1987), 1–5, and "Introduction: A Memoir," in *On Second Thought: A Compilation*, 1–63.

7. Maurice Kenny, "Prelude," in *Between Two Rivers*, 1–5.

8. Kenny, Interview, 28 October 2002.

9. Kenny, *On Second Thought*, 98.

10. Kenny, *Greyhounding This America* (Chico, CA: Heilelberg Graphics, 1988), 20–21:1–25.

11. Kenny, *Last Mornings in Brooklyn: Poems by Maurice Kenny* (Norman, OK: Point Riders Press, 1991), 1:1–4.

12. Kenny, *Greyhounding This America*, 22.

13. Kenny, *On Second Thought*, 100:25–28.

14. Ibid., 102–103:41–42.

15. Kenny, *Carving Hawk: New and Selected Poems, 1953–2000* (Buffalo, NY: White Pine Press, 2002), 51:36–37.

16. Kenny, *On Second Thought*, 86:1–4.

17. Ibid., 70–71.

18. Kenny, *Last Mornings in Brooklyn*, epigraph.

19. Kenny, *Carving Hawk*, 300–301.

20. Interview by author, 28 October 2002.

21. James Ruppert, "The Uses of Oral Tradition in Six Contemporary Native American Poets," *American Indian Culture and Research Journal* 4.1(1980): 89.

22. Kenny, "Land," *North: Poems of Home*: 1–11.

23. Ibid., 60–63.

24. Kenny, *Between Two Rivers* (Fredonia, NY: White Pine Press, 1995), 44:12–13 and 20–22.

25. Kenny, "Our Own Pasts: An Interview with Maurice Kenny," in *Survival This Way: Interviews with Native American Poets*, edited by Joseph Bruchac (Tucson: The University of Arizona Press, 1987), 151–152.

26. Kenny, "Tremolo," *Backward to Forward* (Fredonia, NY: White Pine Press, 1997): 170.

SIX

TORTURED SKINS, BEARS, AND OUR RESPONSIBILITIES TO THE NATURAL WORLD

Nicholle Dragone

After the first reading, Maurice Kenny's collection of short fiction seemed to me to cohere primarily around his critique of colonially imposed assimilation programs and the resulting fragmentation of Indigenous identity. Hence the title, *Tortured Skins and Other Short Fictions*. However, subsequent studies opened this collection up to a culturally based critique through the lens of a Haudenosaunee traditional teachings paradigm. Through this critical lens, Kenny's short fiction functions as twenty-first century allegories about human relationships with and reciprocal responsibilities to all natural world beings, from blackberries, to salmon, to bears, to other humans.

The methodological approach I take in this study of Kenny's short fiction is similar to the approach Cherokee literary critic Chris Teuton demonstrated in his 2008 essay "Theorizing American Indian Literature." This methodology applies oral tradition paradigms to novels, poetry, drama, and other literary works produced by Indigenous authors. In his example, Teuton draws out and contextualizes the concept of "vision," as N. Scott Momaday presents it to his readers in *The Way to Rainy Mountain*, within the very Kiowa oral tradition paradigms that Momaday is engaging with and articulating throughout his book. According to Teuton, there is great potential for Indigenous writers and critics to "develop alternative [theoretical] strategies and critical terms from reading Indigenous literature through the lens of oral tradition paradigms."[1] Again, Teuton eloquently articulates and demonstrates a methodological approach to American Indian literature not unlike the approach I have been working with while studying Seneca / Mohawk poet Maurice Kenny's collection of short stories, *Tortured Skins and other Short Fictions*.[2] The major difference between Teuton's approach and mine is that I am restructuring the critical paradigm to allow me, while standing outside Haudenosaunee culture looking in, to respectfully engage with and critique an Indigenous collection of short fiction that contributes to Haudenosaunee and Indigenous literary canons, as well as to the canons of world and environmental literature.[3] Moreover, by briefly addressing the ecologically grounded message Kenny imparts to his readers through *Tortured Skins;* by contextualizing his "bear" allegories within Haudenosaunee traditional teachings, specifically the Thanksgiving Address and transcribed oral narratives about bears; and by drawing out Kenny's "bears" and showing how he is engaging with and articulating Haudenosaunee traditional teachings about human beings' relationships with and responsibilities to the natural world through his allegorical bear tales, this chapter shows how Kenny has engaged with these traditional teachings to outline his own ecologically grounded message while simultaneously making this message relevant to his twenty-first century reading audiences by weaving it, as a strand of allegorical bear tales, through the warp and woof of the entire tapestry of *Tortured Skins and Other Short Fictions*.

Each of the fourteen short stories Kenny collectively published in *Tortured Skins and Other Short Fiction*, although very different in terms of plot and character development, have been artfully woven together into a single tapestry revolving around an over-arching message. Profoundly relevant in an era when human-induced global climatological change has the potential to devastate ecologies and nations all over world, this message reminds Kenny's readers of their relational accountability, as humans, to the natural world. Furthermore, by weaving this message, as strand of allegorical bear tales, through the warp and woof of the *Tortured Skins* tapestry, Kenny requires his readers to contemplate how much the sociocultural survival of human beings and the ecological survival of the natural world, are absolutely dependent on humans doing the following:

- Recognizing and acknowledging all the elements of the web of creation—blackberries, salmon, bears, humans, waters, mountains, and "birds an' the others"[4]—are our relatives; and,
- Respecting the rights of our human and natural world relatives to survive, now and in the future.

Before contextualizing Kenny's allegorical bear tales within Haudenosaunee traditional teachings, it is important to recognize that he has woven his ecologically based message into and out of each story, ensuring that the entire collection forms a single narrative tapestry speaking to all of his reading audiences, simultaneously, about human responsibilities and relationships not only to each other, but also to all natural world beings.

The first five *Tortured Skins* short fictions discussed here, specifically address the negative impact politics, technology, institutional lifestyles, greed, and passion have on our ability, as humans, to recognize each other's humanity and to respect each other's rights to live in peace and security. "What Did You Say" dramatizes human relationships as mediated through the telephone; whereas "Hammer" comments on the very personal (and often troubled) relationships between college professors and their students. Taken together, these two short stories provide an interesting commentary on the way technology and institutional lifestyles not only isolate us from each other, but also distort and negatively impact the way we relate to each other as humans. "She-Who-Talks-With-Bear," critiques the legacy of the Indian residential school programs in Canada and the United States, a legacy characterized by inability of boarding school survivors to develop and / or maintain healthy emotional and spiritual relationships with their families, home communities, and the natural world.

Furthermore, Kenny bookends all fourteen short stories in the *Tortured Skins*, between two dramatizations of U.S. nineteenth-century military campaigns against Black Kettle's Southern Cheyenne community. These dramatizations, "Black Kettle: Fear and Rescure" and "Forked Tongues," both reflect how nineteenth-century genocidal / ethnocidal practices continue to define the nature of the Southern Cheyenne's relationships, individually, with each other, and collectively, with the U.S. government. Through each of the five stories briefly discussed earlier, we are reminded that our survival as humans often is jeopardized by our inability to see past the politics, technology, institutional lifestyles, greed, and passions isolating us from each other. Once we become isolated, we often are unable or unwilling to recognize each other's humanity. Dehumanizing and othering is the first step on a slippery slope of policies and programs, not unlike Indian residential schools and the nineteenth-century military campaigns waged against the Southern Cheyenne, intending to eradicate ethnicities, peoples, or populations. That Kenny's entire *Tortured Skins* tapestry begins and ends with fictions based on historically documented genocide is itself an interesting authorial commentary on the importance of recognizing our fellow humans as natural world beings whose rights to life deserve to be respected and protected.

In an interesting twist, Kenny moves from discussing human interrelationships to human–natural world relationships, by narrating "Bacon" from the perspective of a couple of bears who are people watching from the relative safety of the woods beyond the clearing. It is the opinion of the bears that the humans theyare watching no longer have any connection to or relationship with the natural world. How else can their disrespectful behavior be explained? Ultimately, the bears' decision to chase this particular group of vacationers out of the woods is rooted in the humans' use of "bear skins" to engage in adult play.

"Blue Jacket," "Visitation," and "Salmon" also present Kenny's readers with bears acting as protagonists and / or antagonists. However, unlike the bears in "Bacon," the bears in all three of these stories, shape-shift into human form with the intent of initiating relationships with their human counterparts. These bear–human interactions force the human characters to interrogate human relationships with and responsibilities to the natural world. "Ohkwa-Ri," "One More," and "Tortured Skins" specifically address the consequences, both to the natural world and to humans, when humans fail to recognize and respect the interdependent, reciprocal relations on which the survival of all natural world beings is predicated. These six stories in particular, are thread of allegorical bear tales, Maurice Kenny has woven into the warp and woof of his *Tortured Skins* narrative. And, as Kenny's allegorical bears inform his readers, once human peoples cease to recognize other natural world peoples as being reciprocally related to them, they have a tendency to reconceive the natural world as objects to be possessed, as resources to be profited from, and, therefore, as expendable. Through the human characters' interactions with bears in "Ohkwa-Ri," "Blue Jacket," "One More," "Salmon," "Visitation," and "Tortured Skins," Kenny not only levels a powerful critique at modern society's recreational exploitation of the natural world, but also affirms Haudenosaunee traditional teachings about human relational accountability to their natural world relations—plants, waters, mountains, humans, animals, and, "the birds an' the others."

Again, although this ecologically grounded message into the fabric of all fourteen short stories comprising the *Tortured Skins and Other Short Fictions* narrative tapestry, Kenny's "bear tales" specifically function as allegories about the importance of remembering, acknowledging, and acting in accordance with our responsibilities to our natural world relations. Furthermore, as Kenny is of Mohawk / Seneca descent, and therefore Haudenosaunee, it can be argued that *Tortured Skins* generally, and Kenny's bear allegories, specifically, are deeply rooted in a distinctly Haudenosaunee traditional teachings paradigm.[5] Before discussing how Kenny is engaging with and articulating Haudenosaunee traditional teachings about humans relationships with and responsibilities to the natural world through his "bears," it is important to briefly contextualize these allegories within the following Haudenosaunee traditional teachings: the Thanksgiving Address and transcriptions of oral narratives about bear–human relations.

The Thanksgiving Address, which is also known in English as either "The Words That Come Before All Else," or the "Original Instructions," is both a traditional teaching and a speech event that continues to have relevance in modern Haudenosaunee life. According to their oral traditions, this speech event was gifted to the Haudenosaunee ancestors by the Skyworld Being who fashioned and breathed life into humans.[6] As a speech event, this particular traditional teaching is the basis of Haudenosaunee ontology and epistemology. To date, it is invoked to open and close all contemporary Haudenosaunee social, political, and cultural gatherings, except funerals. Many Haudenosaunee people meditate on shortened versions of this speech event every morning to greet the new day. And, as this teaching also is known as "The Words That Come Before All Else," it serves to remind the Haudenosaunee that humans, as the youngest element of creation, are related to all other natural world beings, including but not limited to the earth / soil / land, the grasses, the berries and other food or medicine bearing plants, the trees, the waters, the fish, the animals, the birds, the winds and thunders, the sun, moon, and stars, and, ultimately the Creator(s). As an offering of thanksgiving, it acknowledges Haudenosaunee appreciation for the role each natural world being or element plays in human survival. Perhaps, most important, this traditional teaching reminds Haudenosaunee participants that humans relationally accountable to ensure that the delicate balance of life is protected and maintained for the benefit and survival of all future generations—human and nonhuman alike.

Opening and closing all social, political, and cultural gatherings with the Thanksgiving Address, brings the minds of all the participants / listeners together in acknowledgment that if humans, individually or collectively, turn their back on these "Original Instructions," the delicate balance of life that ensures the physical and mental well-being of mankind, as well as the survival of the natural world's coming generations, will be jeopardized.[7] The continued relevance of the Thanksgiving Address in the everyday life, thinking, and epistemology of contemporary Haudenosaunee people, including Kenny, makes this traditional teaching especially important in developing an alternative theoretical framework for critically engaging with all Haudenosaunee-authored literatures.

Furthermore, Kenny's critique, through *Tortured Skins*, on the negative ecological impact human activity has on the natural world, not only engages with the traditional teachings found in the Haudenosaunee Thanksgiving Address, it also articulates the teachings found in Haudenosaunee oral narratives about the interrelationships of humans and bears. There are four Haudenosaunee oral teachings about bears that have particular relevance to Kenny's work: "The Naked Bear," "The Bears That Adopted a Boy,"[8] "The Origin of the Bear Songs and Dances,"[9] and "the Good Hunter."[10] These four stories all describe a time when humans lived in such close connection to the natural world that they were able not only to talk with bears and other animals, but also were able to "shape-shift" into animal form. Likewise, the bears, who are recognized by many North American Indigenous peoples as being closest in physical form and behavior to humans, often took human form to interact with humans.[11] According Haudenosaunee elder Mary Arquette, oral narratives, such as these four, function to remind humans about their kinship with and reciprocal responsibilities to the animals.[12]

According to these traditional teachings, one Haudenosaunee medicine society, together with the associated ceremonies, dances, and songs, were gifted to humans by a family of bears who rescued, adopted, and raised a small boy. While living with the bears, this boy not only learned which forest foods he could eat, but he also was taught dances, songs, and ceremonies still practiced today by one of the Haudenosaunee medicine societies. As these narratives and their corresponding ceremonies inform us, bears are obligated to help humans find medicines when the ceremonies are performed. Humans are reciprocally obligated to perform the bear dances and songs to remind them of "their relationship with animals" and to thank the bears for the medicines and foods bears have gifted to humans.[13]

Like the "adopted boy" stories, the story of the good hunter explains the importance of humans' reciprocal relationships with and responsibilities to the natural world. This narrative tells the story of a hunter whose compassion, generosity, and respect to the animals he hunted resulted in the animals working together to create the medicine necessary to save the hunter's life when they found him laying mortally wounded in the forest. Each animal played a part. The bear "hugged" the wounded hunter "close in his hairy arms" to keep him warm while the other animals completed mixing the medicine necessary to revive the hunter. To honor the animals for their kindness, the Haudenosaunee established a medicine society. Like the medicine society discussed in "adopted boy" narratives, this society is still plays an integral part of Haudenosaunee ceremonial life.[14] Every time these two medicine societies perform the ceremonies, dances, and songs gifted to them by the animals, they are not only honoring the medicines gifted to humans by animals, they are affirming humankind's kinship with and reciprocal responsibilities to each other, to the natural world, and to the coming generations.

Taken together, the Thanksgiving Address, the transcribed versions of these Haudenosaunee bear narratives, and the medicine societies rooted in the bear narratives, are the traditional teachings paradigm in which Kenny's allegorical bear tales are contextualized. Throughout the narrated tapestry of his *Tortured Skins*, Kenny is continuously engaging with, articulating these very Haudenosaunee traditional teachings. Consequently, by drawing out the thread of allegorical bear tales woven so intricately into the warp and woof of *Tortured Skins*, we may better see how Kenny is making the teachings about human kinship with and responsibility to all natural world beings relevant to his twenty-first century reading audiences. Plucking this allegorical thread gently, so as not to destroy narrative tapestry, let us follow it through the following short fictions—"Blue Jacket," "Tortured Skins," "Visitation," "Salmon," "Ohkwa-Ri," and "One More."

"Blue Jacket" and "One More," in particular, affirm that the Haudenosaunee traditional teachings paradigm provides both the context of Kenny's allegorically presented message and an alternative theoretical framework through which Kenny's *Tortured Skins and Other Short Fictions* may be respectfully studied, from outside the culture, by non-Haudenosaunee scholars, such as myself. "Blue Jacket," which is set near the border of Seneca Nation territory in the foothills of the Allegheny Mountains (western New York) is, chronologically, the first of Kenny's allegorical bear tales. From the opening paragraph, this story pulls the reader into the narrator's reminiscences over a conflict he has with the ghost of shape-shifting human over a blackberry patch in his backyard. Through this conflict, the reading audience is introduced to the very same traditional teachings that form the heart of the Haudenosaunee Thanksgiving Address.[15] Likewise, "One More," which is set in the Mohawk Nation's territory in the Adirondack Mountains, opens and closes with the "ancient rhythms" of the Bear Dance.[16] The same dance gifted to the Haudenosaunee in the "adopted boy" oral narratives discussed. Like the traditional teachings paradigm itself, "Blue Jacket" and "One More," work together to speak to Kenny's diverse reading audience humanity's kinship with natural world beings. By virtue of kinship with the natural world humans are, then, reciprocally obligated to acknowledge and offer thanks to the natural world for its life-sustaining gifts. These two stories also speak to Kenny's readers about humanity's relational accountability to the natural world, an accountability that requires humans to ensure their activities not only respect the natural world's rights, but also guarantee the survival of coming generations—human and nonhuman alike. In a very real way, "One More" and "Blue Jacket" become Kenny's allegorical microcosm of the traditional teachings paradigm.

Analytically speaking, these two stories, when read together, function as the knob focusing the lens of a Haudenosaunee-specific traditional teachings paradigmatic framework onto the narrative tapestry of Kenny's *Tortured Skins*. Through this lens, Kenny's underlying ecological message—that there are very real consequences for turning our back on our natural world relations, or by acting in ways that violate their rights—is highlighted and brought to the readers' attention.

Of the many interesting things Kenny does with, "One More," is to insert a quote from the 1993 *Adirondack Daily Enterprise* regarding the compatibility of the Adirondacks' black bear population with "human land uses."

According to this quote, compatibility is ensured by big game hunters who harvest more than six hundred black bears annually.[17] Kenny moves directly from the scientific data rationalizing the annual culling of the black bear population in its own territory into a fictional account of a bear, White Star, who was killed by a reckless tourist. Despite the posted signs warning drivers to "SLOW DOWN / ANIMAL CROSSING," this reckless tourist was racing through the twisting turns and mountains passes of the Adirondacks. Unable to stop in time, he struck White Star with his truck. He jumped out of his truck long enough to shoot the wounded animal, but not long enough to see whether or not his shot put the bear out of its misery.[18] For all intents in purpose this was a hit-and-run "accident." The tourist's actions displayed complete disregard for White Star and her place in the web of life. His actions, likewise, show complete disregard for the bear's right to live safely in her own natural habitats. White Star becomes just another statistic, another bear killed in the exercise of human recreational land uses. In the worldview of the *Adirondack Daily Enterprise*, recreational land uses trump wildlife's rights to life. Consequently, incidents such as these are regrettable, but hardly inappropriate footnotes, in the so-called justifiable culling of wildlife populations.

Through "One More," Kenny not only critiques the needless loss of wildlife to resulting from human recreational land uses, but he also contextualizes this critique through the voice of an old Mohawk man, Henry. Henry's relationship with White Star is symbolic of his life's work to protect the wildlife in the Adirondacks. Throughout the year, he works as both a school custodian and as storyteller / educator teaching children—non-Native and Native—about the natural world. During the early spring, before the forest blossoms back into life, Henry spends a great deal of time providing the birds and animals living with the food necessary to transition from winter's scarcity into summer's bounty. In his capacity as traditional Mohawk man, he participates in the Haudenosaunee Bear Dances and Songs, honoring the bears for their gifts to the Haudenosaunee.

In fact, White Star's story opens and closes to "ancient rhythm" of the Bear Dance, which is described as being older than:

> any of these great conifers or birch or beech of this forest. Nearly as old as these huge granite boulders surging up through the earth, granite boulders tossed into the air by some tremendous volcanic eruption even before his people came to home these mountains and the river lands below. Rhythms certainly older than [Henry . . .].[19]

In opening with these ancient rhythms, "One More," speaks about the importance of passing on these dances and songs to the succeeding generations so that Haudenosaunee youth will always know and respect their bears as their kin. In closing with these same ancient rhythms, "One More," honors the life and mourns the senseless loss of one bear. More than that, by closing "One More" with the ancient rhythms of these ceremonial dances, Kenny seeks to right the imbalance in the web of life resulting when, we as humans, allow our "recreational land use" of places like Adirondacks to trump the rights of wildlife to live in peace and security in their natural habitat.

Although the ancient rhythms of the bear dance are audible in the last few paragraphs of the story, Kenny also takes care to engage with and articulate the Thanksgiving Address through the character of the old Mohawk man. For as Henry drifts off to sleep, he whispers, "Thank you, Great Spirit . . . for the new day."[20] In this way, White Star's life, her friendship with Henry, and her death—defined by the opening quote from the *Adirondack Daily Enterprise* as the culling of wildlife for the benefit of human land uses in the Adirondacks—becomes an allegory for Kenny's diverse reading audience. An allegory engaging with and articulating a distinctly Haudenosaunee traditional teachings paradigm about the importance of recognizing and acknowledging that the rights of wildlife to exist in peace and security, particularly within its own habitat, must be respected and protected—human recreational land use notwithstanding.

Read together, "Blue Jacket," and "One More," highlights Kenny's ability as a modern-day Haudenosaunee storyteller to engage with and draw out an ancient traditional teachings paradigm, and to weave this paradigm into a collection of short stories that simultaneously speaks to the strength and continuity of Haudenosaunee cultural teachings while making those teachings relevant to Kenny's greatly diversified reading audience. Both "One More" and "Blue Jacket" speak to the loss of life and / or the devastation of ecological habitats when human activities prioritize recreational land use and / or ownership claims over the survival of the plants and animals living within a particular ecological niche. Although the action in "Blue Jacket," like the action in "One More," indirectly revolves around a bear, the bear is actually the ghost of an old man, a Seneca elder named Blue Jacket. This ghost shape-shifts back and forth between his human and bear forms in an effort to problematize the narrator's need to hoard the blackberries growing on his property. Contextualized within the Haudenosaunee traditional teachings paradigm, Blue Jacket's ability to shape-shift into a black bear immediately situates this story as an allegorical teaching about the importance of respecting the rights of the natural world.

Despite the fact that Kenny's title character in "Blue Jacket" is a human / bear shape-shifting ghost, this particular short story focuses more on the teachings in the Thanksgiving Address than it does on Haudenosaunee oral narratives on bears. As the self-proclaimed guardian of the blackberry patch, Blue Jacket functions to remind the mixed-blood Mohawk narrator of the lessons his grandparents taught him as a child:

- The "birds an' the others,"[21] depending on the blackberries, are the narrators kinfolk.
- His actions should respect the rights of these natural world beings.
- There are consequences for disrespecting the rights of the "birds an' the others."

In the beginning of the story, it is evident that Blue Jacket's mere presence does, in fact, bring these traditional teachings back to mind. Even before the narrator realizes that Blue Jacket is a ghost, or that the old man has the ability to shape-shift, he informs his readers that Blue Jacket reminds him of his grandparents and their teachings. "But I remember well my grandmother and old Granddad," the narrator tells us, "Mr. Blue Jacket reminds me of Granddad . . . though I was born urban, Grandma and Granddad saw to it I learned a little, at least of the Natural World."[22] He recalls his grandmother taught him that all natural world beings were his kin. Specifically, the moon was his grandmother; the sun, his brother; and, the berries "were sisters."[23] His grandfather taught him to express his appreciation through thanksgiving, "to the Creator and that which has given up its life that you may live . . . elderberry, acorn, or opossum meat."[24] In other words, the message they sought to convey to their grandson is that all living creatures—plants, animals, birds, fish, insects—deserved to be respected because they are humans' natural world relatives. As such, "they too had their rights under the sun the same as we humans."[25]

Despite his fond recollection of these teachings, the narrator emphatically informs his own readers that he was under no obligation to share the blackberries with anyone—not Blue Jacket, not the birds, not any other creature. "It was mine," he insists, "I could let the bloody berry rot if I were so inclined, no?"[26] Every encounter with Blue Jacket further entrenches the narrator in his resolve to be the sole beneficiary of the blackberries growing in his backyard. To ensure this, he erects a four-foot fence all the way around the berry patch.[27]

Our unnamed narrator becomes so obsessed with the blackberries that, despite every outward sign, he is completely unable to recognize the old Seneca shape-shifter for whom, and what he was. On the morning the narrator wakes up to find all his precious blackberries had been harvested right out from under his nose, he follows a trail of Blue Jacket's bear fur and skat from the blackberry patch, up a forested hill, to an old Seneca cemetery. The skat and fur tufts lead him directly to a tombstone smeared with blackberry juice. To his chagrin and horror, the tombstone reads: "Blue Jacket, Seneca 1829."[28]

Given the role of "bear narratives" in the Haudenosaunee traditional teachings paradigm, you might think Kenny's nameless narrator would recognize that Blue Jacket's true identity—as both a ghost of a long-dead Seneca elder, and a shape-shifting bear—was a gift. A gift to help restore balance to his mind and life by reminding him the traditional teachings he learned as a child continue to be relevant to his life. However, the nameless narrator's mind became so unbalanced by his obsession with the blackberries and by his need to see the blackberries as objects subject to his ownership that the narrator was unable to acknowledge the blackberries as his kin. Nor was he able to recognize or accord the blackberries and the animals depending on the blackberries for survival with the same rights to life he exercised for himself.

In fact, the moment he realized the truth about Blue Jacket's identity, the narrator's obsession with the blackberries was transformed into a consuming fear of Old Blue Jacket. The blackberries became the physical manifestation of his irrational fear of human–bear shapeshifters. After all, according to his own culture's traditional teachings, shapeshifters function as messengers bringing gifts and / or teaching lessons necessary to ensure the survival of the future generations. Unable to rap his mind around the reality of these teachings, and their physical manifestation through Blue Jacket and the blackberries, the narrator promptly ripped out the entire blackberry patch, roots and all, and burned them.

The irony is that this action clarified how far removed the narrator had become from himself, as a Mohawk man. Through his wanton destruction of the blackberries, he again rejected his grandparents' teachings that the berries were his sisters, and, as such, deserved their rights to life be respected. Understood through the lens of the traditional teachings paradigm, "Blue Jacket's" narrator effectively murders his own sisters. A crime of passion. And, once the berries have been ripped out by their roots and burned, the narrator spends the rest of the summer locked away his study. To his reading audience, he rationalizes his actions—the destruction of the berries, isolating himself away from the natural world, and his refusal to eat berries of any kind, ever again—as an all consuming fear of ghosts and / or bears.

Together, "One More," and "Blue Jacket," affirm that Kenny, as a Haudenosaunee storyteller, has engaged with and articulated Haudenosaunee traditional teachings about man's kinship with and responsibilities to the natural world through his collection of short stories. Specifically, by articulating this message allegorically through bear tales such as "Blue Jacket" and "One More," which are, themselves, contextualized in Haudensoaunee oral traditions, Kenny has masterfully created an analytical framework for respectfully studying this entire collection of short stories while, standing as I do, outside Haudenosaunee culture, looking in. Furthermore, these two stories become the knob focusing the lens of this Haudenosaunee-specific paradigmatic framework on Kenny's other allegorical bear tales—"Tortured Skins," "The Visitation," "Salmon," and "Ohkwa-Ri."

Like the story line in Kenny's "One More," both "Tortured Skins," and "Ohkwa-Ri," revolve around human recreational land use and its negative impact on the black bears' Adirondacks ecology. Unlike, "One More," however, it is not the bear that pays the ultimate price for man's recreational land use choices. Rather, it is man who suffers the consequences when recreational land use conflicts with the bears' rights to survive within their ecological niche. In "Tortured Skins," mixed-blood Abenaki protagonist Rudy Peregrin, obsessed with hunting Adirondack bears into extinction, meets a gruesome and untimely demise in the arms of black bear. "Ohkwa-Ri," which focuses on the poaching of black bears, reaches its climax when the poacher and the bears' self-proclaimed protector kill each other in a stand-off over the bears. In both stories, the attempts of poachers and hunters to either exterminate or cull the bear population in the Adirondacks results, ironically, in the culling of the human "recreationist" population. Man pays the ultimate price for seeking to rationalize actions threatening the black bears' survival with the excuse of recreational land use. It is as if the Bear Dance performed by Old Henry in "One More," has reset the balance of life in the Adirondacks by turning the tables on the sportsmen and the poachers.

Through "Ohkwa-Ri," "One More," and "Tortured Skins," Kenny engages with and articulates Haudenosaunee traditional teachings on humanity's kinship with and responsibilities to the natural world. The bears in each of these stories serve as allegories for the ecologically based message Kenny teases out of these traditional teachings and imparts to his readers. Specifically, Kenny's bears, as symbolic of all natural world beings, are to be understood and recognized as human beings' close relatives. As such, their rights to life and habitat are to protected and respected, not jeopardized by human activities. Furthermore, as the disrespecting or ignoring of the rights of natural world beings in three bear allegories results in the unnecessary deaths of humans and bears, Kenny's diverse reading audiences—Haudenosaunee, Indigenous, world literature and environmental literature—are provided with serious food for thought about the consequences of prioritizing human recreational privileges over the natural world's rights to life.

In each story, the consequences, however unintended, are horrifyingly possible. Animals, like White Star, are killed every day by careless drivers careening through mountain passes of wildlife preserves and national parks. Like Kenny's mixed-blood protagonist Rudy Peregrin, more hunters than we realize are killed by the very animals they hope to bag and tag. Sadly, like the bears in "Ohkwa-Ri," animals are killed every day by poachers hoping to profit from the price of the hide. Sometimes, as in this story, poachers pay the ultimate consequence for their illegal activities at the hands of vigilantes and game wardens. Each of these three stories stands as allegory for humankind's place within the web of life. Our place within that web defines us as inextricably related to all other creatures and plants. Actions jeopardizing the delicate balance of life represented by this web, threaten the future survival not just of our natural world relations, but also of ourselves. Furthermore, by our very kinship with natural world beings, we are obligated, not only to acknowledge, but to respect the rights of the natural world. If we choose, as careless tourists, as greedy poachers, as obsessed hunters, or, as in the case of "Blue Jacket's" nameless narrator, as rigid land owners, to act in ways that jeopardize or deny the rights of the natural world, the consequences, as Kenny's allegorical bears remind, us, may be devastating for both human and natural world beings alike. Kenny's genius as a modern-day Haudenosaunee storyteller is further reinforced by the way he teases out and articulate his ecologically based message through two tales shape-shifting bears and / or humans. Like "Blue Jacket," the shape-shifters in "Visitation," and "Salmon," force the people they interact with to rethink their place within the natural order, their kinship with the natural world, and / or their reciprocal responsibilities to natural world beings.

"Salmon," the last of Kenny's allegorical bear tales, again presents readers with a conflict between natural world beings' rights to life and human privileges to use land, water, and even fish, for recreational activities.[29] The action in "Salmon" revolves around a group of men recreationally fishing along the banks of Sandy Creek in upstate New York. As the day progressed, the men complained bitterly that they had paid fifteen dollars to fish at this location and not single one of them had angled any salmon.[30]

Throughout the day, Joe, one of the men in this group of would-be sportsmen, was consistently preoccupied by the dark figures watching the men from both bridge above them and the thick brush lining the shore. When these dark figures being ambling down to the river bank, the fishermen realized these figures weren't human at all, they were bears. Most of the men quickly scattered, racing back up hill to the relative safety of their vehicles. A few, however, including Joe, stripped down to red breech cloths and joined the bears. Within moments the bears waded into the water, spearing countless salmon with their claws.

When they stopped to catch their breath, the men were shocked and horrified to find that two of their friends had joined the bears in the river. They were equally horrified to discover that the farmer whose land they paid fifteen dollars per head to fish on had shape-shifted into a bear. They watched as their friends, the bears, and the shape-shifting farmer pulled one salmon after another out of the same river that moments before seemed to be devoid all fish life.

According to the Haudenosaunee Thanksgiving Address, the fish, like other natural world beings, were instructed by the Creator to perform certain duties, including offering themselves up to as food to sustain humans, bears, and other animals.[31] Humans, likewise, were instructed about their reciprocal responsibilities to the fish:

1. to ensure that the water quality of the lakes, rivers, and oceans supports the reproduction and survival of the fish; and,
2. to ensure ecological balance is maintained by abstaining from overfishing, commercially, recreationally, or otherwise.

Although the sportsmen fishing at Sandy Creek readily acknowledged they had no intention of eating the fish they caught, they spent hours trying hook, net, and snag as many salmon as possible. On the other hand, the bears are in the stream but a few minutes before they spear just enough fish to sustain themselves. If we, as Kenny's reading audience, stand back with the fishermen on the hills above of Sandy Creek, and watch the bears and humans feasting together on "Salmon," we quickly realize there is no hierarchy among the men and bears. Each makes room for the others along the river banks. Each partakes equally in the day's catch. If we contextualize Kenny's "Salmon" in the teachings of the Thanksgiving Address, then it can be argued that the fish, recognizing their reciprocal relations to their human and bear relatives, gave themselves only to those beings—human and bears—whose actions honored this reciprocal relationship.

The action in "Visitation," like "Salmon," and "Blue Jacket," revolves around a bear–human shape-shifter. In Haudenosaunee oral tradition, there are three types of shape-shifters. As noted in the two stories about the bears adopting a human boy, the first are animals who shape-shift into human form to bring humans messages and / or gifts. The second are humans who shape-shift into animal form to accomplish a task using the strengths of that particular animal. In the story of the "The Naked Bear," the runners chosen to initiate peace between two neighboring villages use their ability to shape-shift into either an owl or a wolf, to move more quickly, between the villages than they otherwise could in their human forms.

The third type of shape-shifter is a spirit, sometimes the Creator himself, who takes on human form to see if humans are conducting themselves in accordance with the original instructions laid out in Thanksgiving Address. Although not discussed previously, the most relevant traditional teaching discussing this type of shape-shifter explains how the Haudenosaunee bear clan became the "Keepers of Medicine." Briefly, in this story, the Creator takes on the form of a sick old stranger, wandering from longhouse to longhouse seeking food and lodging. The clan mother of each longhouse turns him away without any aid until he arrives at the very last longhouse in the village—the longhouse of the bear clan. Remembering the teachings of the Thanksgiving Address, the clan mother takes it on herself not only to welcome the old man into the longhouse, but to also feed, clothe, and care for him until his health is restored.[32] To honor her hospitality and good-mindedness, the Creator reveals himself to her, promising that the bear clan would forever be known as the "Keepers of Medicine."[33]

This oral narrative, combined with the Haudenosaunee narratives about the bears who adopted the boy, are particularly relevant in studying the way Kenny engages with and articulates Haudenosaunee traditional teachings about humanity's relationships with and responsibilities to the natural world through his short story "Visitation." As in "Salmon" and "Blue Jacket," the shape-shifter in "Visitation" takes on the role of messenger, speaking to the humans he interacts with about the importance of sharing nature's bounty among all natural world being.[34] However, the shape-shifter in "Visitation" differs from Farmer Jones in "Salmon" and the ghost of the long-dead Seneca elder in "Blue Jacket" in that he does not appear to be a human (or ghost of a human) possessed of a power to transform into a bear. Rather, in "Visitation," the shape-shifter is either a bear or a Creator spirit, who has taken on human form as a convenience for interacting with the Mohawk people living on the Akwesasne reserve in northern New York. Interestingly, this bear, like the bears in Kenny's "Bacon" and "Salmon," watches humans for quite some time before revealing himself to them.

The shape-shifting bear in Kenny's "Visitation," like the Creator spirit in the Haudenosaunee traditional teaching explaining how the bear clan became the medicine keepers, has taken on the form of a travel-weary stranger. Walking from house to house, in the bush of the Akwesasne Mohawk reservation, this stranger seeks hospitality only to be rejected time and time again. At long last he finds himself enjoying a simple meal of cold soup and bread with honey, while visiting with an elderly Mohawk couple—Monroe and Agnes Bond. During this dinner, the shape-shifter slowly reveals his true form to the Bonds. Transforming into a bear before their eyes, he tells them that they alone, of all the people he interacted with in the Akwesasne Bush, remembered their obligations, as outlined in traditional teachings, to "offer a taste of [their] labors and harvest to [him]."[35] Consequently, he is duty-bound to both accept and reciprocate their hospitality and kindness to him.

As he ambles toward the Bonds' door, the shape-shifting stranger slowly transforms from a bear back into a swarthy, travel-weary man. Turning to leave their cabin, the stranger tells the Bonds that because of their kindness to him, they need not fear anything. Not the dark or the night. Not any creature that walks the dark night, the early dawn, or high noon. Not even the recent crime wave gripping the reserve. He will be watching them, protecting them.[36] Thus, through "Visitation," Kenny reminds his readers that just as there are consequences for turning our back on our duties to share the bounties of creation with our natural world relations, there also are positive repercussions for fulfilling our obligations to and respecting the rights of our human and nonhuman relatives.

Throughout *Tortured Skins and Other Short Fictions*, Kenny contextualized an ecologically grounded message about humanity's relationships with and responsibilities to the natural world within the traditional teachings of his own Haudenosaunee culture. Although all fourteen short fictions collected and published in this volume talk about the importance of respecting the rights of life belonging to all natural world beings—from blackberries to bears to humans—Kenny specifically articulates this ecologically grounded message through seven "bear" tales. Each of these bear tales function, allegorically, to remind us, as humans, that we are kin to all natural world beings—human and nonhuman alike. By virtue of this kinship, we are accountable for ensuring that our relations' rights to live and to thrive within their own ecological niche are respected, not jeopardized by our actions. Likewise, the shape-shifting bears in Kenny's "Salmon," "Blue Jacket," and "Visitation" remind us that natural world beings—bears, salmon, blackberries, and humans—are obligated to reciprocate our kindness and hospitality to them by giving of themselves to ensure that both we, and the other natural world beings making up the web of Creation, will survive together into the coming generations and beyond. On the other hand, "One More," "Ohkwa-Ri," and "Tortured Skins" stand as a warning that jeopardizing the survival of any element of the natural world by prioritizing human privilege to use land recreationally over natural world beings' rights to life can, and very often will, result in tragedy. The deaths of the bear poacher and the vengeful hunter in "Ohkwa-Ri" and "Tortured Skins," remind us that the consequences of denying our relationship with and responsibilities to the natural world may even include the loss of human life.

Kenny, as a modern-day Haudenosaunee storyteller, has engaged with the Haudenosaunee traditional teachings paradigm, contextualized his collection of short fiction in this paradigm, and provided his readers with a critical methodology enabling them to recognize the significance of Kenny's literary contributions to Haudenosaunee canons, as well as the canons world and environmental literature. Again, to accomplish this, he has drawn out the underlying message of the Haudenosaunee Thanksgiving Address and oral narratives about bear–human interrelationships, and has woven that message as an allegorical thread into warp and woof of his narrative tapestry *Tortured Skins and Other Short Fictions*. Separately, and together, Kenny's allegorical bear tales take Haudenosaunee teachings about human kinship with and responsibilities to the natural world and transform them into an ecologically grounded message accessible to all of his reading audiences. Consequently, in era when human-induced global warming has the potential to jeopardize the survival of humans and nonhumans alike, Kenny's ecologically grounded, Haudenosaunee-contextualized message about acknowledging our kinship with the natural world, have just as meaning for readers of environmental and world literatures as it does for the readers of Indigenous literatures. The tapestry of Maurice Kenny's *Tortured Skins and Other Short Fictions* is but one example of a literary genius that has contributed and will continue to contribute to a wide variety of literary canons, including the Haudenosaunee, Indigenous, world and environmental literary canons.

> "I came only for a glass of water. I was dusty and thirsty. You good people gave me water and cold soup. You quenched my thirst and added the surprise of the soup and the bread with the honey and butter. No one else on this road welcomed me in for drink or food. . . . How could I not come in and accept the glass of water, the bowl of soup, and this bread? It was my duty, as it was your duty to have these things and to offer a taste of your labors and harvest to me."
>
> —"Visitation," from *Tortured Skins and Other Short Fictions*

> "What's your name, Not-so-much-Indian?"
>
> He didn't stop to hear my reply.
>
> "My Maud was the one who said I talked too much. If I worked the way I talked, I'd get the work done. Why hell, damn. I don't want to know your name. You got a name now: Not-so-much-Indian. I only wanna know if you'll share these blackberries when you buy this house. Share with the birds, an' the others."
>
> —"Blue Jacket," from *Tortured Skins and Other Short Fictions*

NOTES

1. In his essay, "Theorizing American Indian Literature: Applying Oral Concepts to Written Traditions," Cherokee literary critic Chris Teuton points out

that there is great potential for indigenous literary critics and writers to "develop alternative strategies and critical terms from reading Native literature through the lens of oral traditional paradigms" (209–214).

2. Teuton's approach looks at the way alternative methodological strategies and critical terms can be drawn out of indigenous literatures that are contextualized within oral tradition paradigms from which the literature has grown. My approach, in this chapter, looks at Kenny's discussion of bears as being allegorical in nature, "bears as nature" if you will. As Teuton does with the alternative strategies and critical terms he draws out of Indigenous Literature, I too am contextualizing Kenny's allegorical bears within the Haudenosaunee oral tradition paradigms they grew out of.

3. As alluded to previously, before undertaking such a culturally based interpretation of Maurice Kenny's *Tortured Skins*, it is important to acknowledge that although I have had the great good fortune not only to grow up near Haudenosaunee communities, but also to mature under the guidance of several Haudenosaunee elders, I am writing this chapter standing outside Haudenosaunee culture looking in. I am of Dakota/Lakota descent but am not enrolled in any of the Dakota/Lakota communities in the United States or Canada. Therefore, I am not a citizen of the Great Sioux Nation or any other First Nations community. Additionally, it must also be acknowledged that by engaging with and critiquing Kenny's text as a cultural outsider, I was working solely with transcribed versions of Haudenosaunee traditional teachings, including the Thanksgiving Address, Creation, and oral narratives regarding bears. Thus, in keeping with the philosophy of the Thanksgiving Address, which tells us that, "we must always remember that we are not perfect, that we can and will make mistakes . . . we must acknowledge these errors for they reflect our responsibilities to the" the people and the natural world—I take the opportunity here, to do just that. Any mistakes I have made in interpreting Haudenosaunee traditional teachings are my own. Furthermore, it also is important here, for me as literary critic, to acknowledge that I have a responsibility to those peoples whose literary works with which I am critically engaged. That said, it is my sincere desire that this chapter not only honor those Haudenosaunee elders to whom I am relationally accountable, but also that this chapter may contribute to the development of one potential methodology for critically engaging indigenous literary texts respectfully from outside the culture in which the text was produced.

4. Kenny, Maurice. "Blue Jacket," in *Tortured Skins and Other Short Fictions*. (East Lansing: Michigan State University Press, 2000) 25–46, 29.

5. The Haudenosaunee, also known as the People of the Longhouse and the Iroquois, are comprised of six nations of peoples: the Mohawk, the Oneida, the Onondaga, the Cayuga, the Seneca, and the Tuscarora Nations.

6. "Johe:koh—The Sustainers of Life," in *Iroquois Creation Story: John Arthur Gibson and J.N.B. Hewitt's Myth of the Earth Grasper*, ed. John C. Mohawk (Buffalo, NY: Mohawk Publications, 2005), 77–80.

7. For more information on the Haudenosaunee Thanksgiving Address, please see the Haudenosaunee Environmental Task Force's 1999 publication titled, *Words that Come Before All Else. Environmental Philosophies of the Haudenosaunee*. Also, please see *The Great Peace: the Gathering of the Good Minds* CD-ROM (Working World Training Centre, 1998); Michael Foster and Jake Thomas in *From the Earth*

to Beyond the Sky: An Ethnographic Approach to Four Longhouse Iroquois Speech Events (Ottawa: National Museum of Man, 1974); J. N. B. Hewitt in *Iroquoian Cosmology (First book)*, (Washington DC: U.S. Government Printing Office, 1904); J. N. B. Hewitt in *Iroquoian Cosmology, Part II* (New York: AMS Press, 1974); D. Longboat, "*Owehna' shon:a (The Islands). The Haudenosaunee Archipelago: The Nature and Necessity of Bio-Cultural Restoration and Revitalizatio*," (PhD Diss., York University, 2008); and, John C. Mohawk, "Foreword," in *Iroquois Creation Story: John Arthur Gibson and J.N.B. Hewitt's Myth of the Earth Grasper* (Buffalo, NY: Mohawk Publications, 2005).

8. "The Naked Bear," and "The Bears That Adopted a Boy," were both transcribed Seneca Storyteller Jesse J. Cornplanter, in letter form to a non-Native friend. Eventually they were published by Cornplanter in a collection title *Legends of the Longhouse*. Originally published in 1938, this collection was republished in the *Iroquois Reprints* series by Iroqrafts in 1992.

J. J. Cornplanter in *Legends of the* Longhouse. (Ohsweken: Iroqrafts, 1992), 89–122; 151–165.

9. Working together with Jeremiah Curtin, Tuscarora Ethnologist J. N. B Hewitt and Jeremiah Curtin, transcribed this oral narrative and published it with hundreds of other Haudenosaunee oral narratives through the Bureau of Ethnology in 1918.

J. N. B. Hewitt and Jeremiah Curtin, ed. in *Seneca Fiction, Legends and Myths 1910–1911*. Part II (Washington DC: U.S. Government Printing Office, 1918), 658–663.

10. Working together with Harriet Maxwell Converse, Seneca anthropologist Arthur C. Parker transcribed this version of "The Good Hunter," in 1908. It was republished in 1981 by the State University of New York Press. Arthur C. Parker and Harriet Maxwell Converse, ed. in *Myths and Legends of the New York Iroquois*. (Albany: The University of the State of New York, 1981), 150–156.

11. Cornplanter 151–165; Hewitt and Curtin 658–663.

12. Arquette, Mary, "The Animals," in *Words That Come Before All Else . . .*, ed. Haudenosaunee Environmental Task Force (Cornwall, NY: Native North American Traveling College, 1999), 82–101.

13. Arquette, "The Animals," 88; Hewitt and Curtin 660, 663.

14. Arthur C. Parker and Harriet Maxwell Converse, ed. in *Myths and Legends of the New York Iroquois*. (Albany: State University of New York Press, 1981), 150–156.

15. Kenny, Maurice. "Blue Jacket," in *Tortured Skins and Other Short Fictions*. (East Lansing: Michigan State University Press, 2000) 25–46.

16. Kenny, Maurice. "One More," in *Tortured Skins and Other Short Fictions*. (East Lansing: Michigan State University Press, 2000) 149–162.

17. Kenny, "One More," 149.

18. Ibid., 154, 159.

19. Ibid., 150.

20. Ibid., 160–162.

21. Kenny, "Blue Jacket," 29.

22. Ibid., 30–31.

23. Ibid., 31.

24. Ibid.

25. Ibid.

26. Ibid., 29.

27. Ibid., 40.

28. Ibid., 45.

29. Kenny, Maurice. "Salmon," in *Tortured Skins and Other Short Fictions* (East Lansing: Michigan State University Press, 2000) 163–169.

30. Kenny, "Salmon," 166–168.

31. Patterson, Neal. "The Fish," in *Words That Come Before All Else . . .* , ed. Haudenosaunee Environmental Task Force (Cornwall: Native North American Traveling College, 1999), 44–50.

32. Arquette, "The Animals," 89.

33. Tehanetorens, "The Gift of the Great Spirit," in *Tales of the Iroquois, Volumes I and II*. (Ohsweken: Iroqrafts, Ltd., 1992. 34–40, 40.

34. Kenny, Maurice. "Visitation," in *Tortured Skins and Other Short Fictions* (East Lansing: Michigan State University Press, 2000) 69–90.

35. Kenny, "Visitation," 85–86.

36. Ibid., 86.

SEVEN

TEACHING MAURICE KENNY'S FICTION

Dislocated Characters, Narrators, and Readers

Alan Steinberg and Karen Gibson

The first piece of writing in Maurice Kenny's short story collection, *Tortured Skins and Other Fictions*, features a shifting collage of dreams, visions, and prophecies concerning the 1868 Battle of Washita River. Chief Black Kettle, who was killed during the massacre, provides one perspective of the days leading up to the battle, whereas a host of other characters, both historical and fictional, lend their own take on this traumatic event. Among the characters who speculate on the fate of both themselves and their tribe is Monahsetah, a Cheyenne woman who was captured during the attack and has gone down in history for later giving birth to a child who was possibly fathered by George Armstrong Custer. Days before the battle, Monahsetah contemplates the life of all 'half-breeds': "They lived in two worlds, half-breeds, never really a part of either, and they were considered as much a cur, a mongrel, as any half-wolf camp dog."[1] Both Monahsetah and Black Kettle seem aware of the impending doom, yet they lack the full knowledge or the power to alter it. Nevertheless, their richly descriptive yet fragmented musings provide a humane contrast to the cold documents of extermination authored by Custer, Sherman, and others, also included in the story.

Native American writing has long been known for this technique of narrative fragmentation, from early biographies that defied European expectations by focusing more on the life of the tribe than that of an individual to contemporary fiction that attempts to revise the reader's suppositions regarding historical positivism by suggesting other possibilities through multiple perspectives, magical occurrences, and mythical events. Native American history not only is inseparable from the oral tradition in which it has been kept alive, a tradition steeped in story and metaphor, it has often partly been lost through fragmentation and dispersal. Its recreation means fitting those pieces back together, wherever one might find them, and "Black Kettle: Fear and Recourse" uses this method to achieve both drama and dislocation, perspective and lost possibilities, and serves as an inviting prelude to the stories that follow. In reference to his Molly Brant poems, Kenny has said that he is committed to reshaping "some historical inaccuracies or lies into a semblance of at least poetic truth, if not recorded fact."[2] Against the grain of those who contend that history is fact and fact is truth, many of the stories in *Tortured Skins* extend the range of this "poetic truth," using shifting narrative perspective in a manner that often seems to match Kenny's own position within the Native community, one of contention and sometimes alienation.

Anyone who has attempted to make Indigenous literature part of the curriculum knows the special challenges it can present.[3] Non-native students initially may have trouble identifying and making sense of the symbolism used by Native writers. Further complicating this issue, meanings for these symbols may actually shift depending on tribe, locality, and any number of other issues that separate and diversify Native cultures. Dealing with shifting signifiers as well as shifting narrative perspectives might be frustrating for some students, but it also can offer a rewarding challenge. As the students work to "fit" the story together, they can understand and appreciate more fully the complex history, mythology, and symbolism of Native American cultures.

When we use Kenny's story "Visitation" in class, students generally are quick to pick up on the importance of the narrative perspective. The story is about the relationship between an elderly couple, Agnes and Monroe, who have spent their lives on the reservation. One night while eating dinner their home is visited by a young man. Monroe asks the young man to join them, despite Agnes's reluctance. As they share their simple meal, Agnes begins to notice that their visitor is slowly transforming into a rough and hairy creature resembling a black bear. At the same time, Monroe, who has been blind for several years, seems to be regaining his sight. The essential point that students quickly pick up on is that the story is told from the point of view of Agnes, not Monroe, and Agnes is afraid. Rather than welcoming the bear spirit into their home and celebrating the gifts he brings, she wants to shut him out, especially to deny his gifts and the spirits of the ancestors out of fear that she will be asked to join them. If Monroe had been telling the story, students point out, they would have viewed the bear's visit differently. Monroe, perhaps because of his blindness, is much more open to the wonderful magic offered by their visitor. In this simple observation lies the power of Kenny's fiction. As often as readers are invited to witness a world of natural forces and Native symbolism, they remain uneasy visitors in this space.

The non-Native reader, especially, is forced into the awkward position of witnessing events that he or she either fears or must struggle to understand. This technique is perhaps best exemplified in "The Girl on the Beach," a key story in this collection. A middle-aged man, non-Native, is vacationing at a resort in Mexico. While there, he repeatedly sees a young girl on the beach. At least she initially appears to be a young girl. Each time he sees or speaks to the girl, she grows older. Also, inconveniently for the man, she insists on revealing unpleasant details about her life: the abuse by her stepfathers, her life as a prostitute in the city. As embarrassing as this is for the tourist, the reader also is forced to live through his confusion and unease. Like him, the reader is both intrigued and repelled by the girl and all that she exposes about culture—the degradation and exploitation of others, as well as other unspeakable qualities. Where do we stand in this equation? For example, when the girl introduces herself in the lobby of the hotel, the student, as reader, along with the tourist must puzzle through her presentation of self:

> "But I am India."
>
> "What do you mean . . . India, if it is not your name nor where you come from?"
>
> . . . "I am India. I am Olmec."
>
> "Olmec?" He was not only puzzled, but totally confused.
>
> "Yes, yes. Olmec. India. I am an Olmec Indian. From Mexico. The state of . . ."[4]

As unreliable as the young girl's tales of her life might appear, by the end of the story students also must accept the unreliability of the narrator as well. When the other guests at the hotel / resort give their own version of his story in the police report, we begin to doubt the very existence of the girl:

> "He was weird," the young man who served as bartender said, shaking his head. "He came to the bar one night, and sat there talking to himself and getting the answer."[5]

Another worker at the hotel, a waitress, reports: "And he was cheap, believe me. He pinched me one morning at breakfast, my butt, and he had the goddamn gall to tip me a quarter."[6] Is the girl the embodiment of the man's worst fears and most abject desires? Or is he hers? Or ours? One thing that seems certain is that as readers, we are faltering on this same plane of uncertainty. Students struggle with this dislocation. They want easy answers and stories that unfold in familiar territory. If the story does not provide this, their first impulse is to offer their own "reasonable" explanations: The man on the beach is crazy; Agnes hallucinates the bear's visit, a side effect of her arthritis medication. In time, however, and with some background information, they become more comfortable with the language of visions and symbols and learn to navigate this landscape, perhaps even connecting it to such modern literary traditions as magic realism and deconstruction.

In this story, too, the narrative perspective shifts, if only slightly, from time to time, forcing the reader to question the tourist's depiction and understanding of events long before the ending. While the entire story is told from a third-person point of view, most of the events are recounted using the tourist's perspective: "Now he could observe her better and discovered her skin was a beautiful cinnamon color, tanned to perfection."[7] Yet at times, the narrative voice becomes more speculative: "He must have thought that a grand idea, to take the chair beside the young girl. May I, he might have asked her, before sitting himself."[8] Again, the uncertainty: Did it really happen this way? Or is it all speculation? Like the young man in "Visitation," the girl on the beach is a vehicle of transformation, and like the bear he transforms into, she forces us to question the power and the significance of that transformation. Students, whose lives are essentially made up of a series of transformations—from underclassmen to upperclassmen; from legal dependents to adults—find this aspect of "shifting realities" especially relevant and engaging once they open themselves to its possibility in fiction.

Kenny returns to this bear metaphor, both as trickster and as a symbol of what is lost, many times throughout the collection. The bear often is the victim of outside forces, and it also is the one thing to which the characters relate, without understanding why. In "One More," the main character is comfortable with his life and fairly knowledgeable about both nature and his own heritage. His grandson is a traditionalist who is preparing for "the ceremony in the Longhouse"; his wife cooks many of the same meals enjoyed by their ancestors; and the main character himself feeds and cares for creatures of the woods with respect and genuine affection. All this, however, does not prevent the ugliness of "civilization" from disrupting their world when a passing motorist thoughtlessly kills one of his bears.

Another potent example of Native traditions clashing with "civilization" can be found in the character Mary Margaret in the story "She-Who-Speaks-With-Bear." Mary Margaret is a young Native girl who has been confined in a convent school. Years before, her grandmother had given her a bear's claw that allows Mary Margaret to communicate with the bear spirit. When bear speaks to her, however, offering information about her mother's illness and impending death, it makes the young girl's situation worse rather than better, since she is unable to escape the convent for one last visit with her mother. In this story the reader begins to glimpse the painful desocialization process as a young character is ripped from the context of her ancestral heritage and forced to live in an alien and often hostile environment. Kenny's negatively rendered images of the convent auditorium where she is being punished speak to the desolate hopelessness of the character's situation: "A room or a place without a June breeze, a meadow lark's trill, the scent of clover or wild milkweed; a room without a candle, lantern, or at least a flashlight to search corners, or a crack of moon falling under the door or across the transit is eternity,"[9] and Mary Margaret's shriek of agony is the only reasonable response to her situation: "A growl wrenched from Mary Margaret's very essence, her spirit, her heart, her brain. Her scream shrilled through the auditorium, echo after echo filled the hall, reverberating. It drummed through the corridor beyond the opened door."[10] For Mary Margaret this is a transitional space, one she is lucky enough to escape eventually, but not without permanent scars. We learn at the end of the story that she "still hears those screams in Montana, her home, as she continues to speak to Bear."[11]

While Mary Margaret has some knowledge of her cultural heritage on her side, other characters are not so lucky. On the other hand, the main character knows he is part Native American, but little more than that: "Their parents hid from their tribal affiliations, and consequently when Patrick came into the world and was old enough to start learning exactly who he was, his parents could not tell him what his Indian blood was. They just didn't know."[12] Despite his lost heritage, however, Patrick seems at some level to understand that he is a member of the bear clan, and must protect these animals: "I don't know. I just don't know, but a voice keeps saying, 'You don't kill bear.' "[13] Throughout the story his protective instincts grow, apparently without what we might call understanding, and at the end, he is seriously wounded when he confronts a hunter, the killer of several innocent bears. Patrick's wife, Colette, observes the events, innocent of his motivations and shocked by his injuries as well as his part in the drama. As vaguely as Patrick understands his instincts, his wife understands them even less because they defy any explanation he might give her. Although most of the story has been told from Patrick's perspective, in the end we observe the events with Colette's bewilderment and shock.

Tradition plays a vital role in these stories, yet tradition is continually disrupted and challenged. The reader observes as an onlooker, sympathetic, but powerless and only half comprehending. When the narrator briefly allows some insight through a character's perspective, it is only to snatch it away again in the next paragraph. If the reader's non-Native status is problematic for interpreting events, the characters' half-breed status seems to be even more at issue. In her essay "A Stranger in My Own Life: Alienation in Native American Prose and Poetry" Paula Gunn Allen remarks that "the ancient thrust toward unification with the people is not lost in modern Indian literature. But it is a painful urge, one that is beset by isolation, powerlessness, denial, pain and loss of self; it is one that is often worked out violently."[14] Allen quotes extensively from Kenny's poetry to show that "Alienation, as a theme, is more than a literary device in these works. It is an articulation of a basic experience, one that is characteristic of the life and consciousness of the half-breed."[15] Kenny has firsthand experience with this double sense of belonging and exclusion. His early life was divided between Brooklyn and Watertown (upstate New York) with occasional visits to Canada, where many of his relatives lived. In each of these places, and many more throughout his life, the "purity" of his heritage was questioned. In his autobiographical memoir he notes: "The world does not seem to want to accept the blood quantum I have in the veins. I'm always being questioned. My work is saturated with poems dealing with this theme. What is an Indian . . . blood, heart, spirit, colour?"[16] In his fiction, half-breed status often leads the characters into situations they do not fully understand, and where they perform awkwardly, as in Patrick's case.

Perhaps one reason students relate so well to these stories is that they too, at least temporarily, inhabit a transitional space and time. As college freshmen, they leave behind a familiar world where they are known and where they know how to respond. Leaving this behind can be a disconcerting experience. Then as students they are asked to shoulder the responsibilities of adults, while still being treated as children. They must perform competently in their work while the reward of mastery status is always delayed, and while they may become fairly comfortable participants in one class, there is always another class where they are neophytes. Although Kenny's stories don't always provide happy, safe endings to their existential uncertainties, they do give the student reader the comfort of knowing others have walked, or perhaps fearfully shuffled, these same shadowy paths. As Kenny writes in a poem entitled "You Know Who You Are, Were, Will Be:"

> . . . remember
> the shine of the words / magic
> dangling on moonlight
> always—[17]

NOTES

1. Maurice Kenny, *Tortured Skins and Other Fictions* (East Lansing: Michigan State University Press, 1999), 2.

2. Arnold Krupat, "American Histories, Native American Narratives," *Early American Literature* 30 (1995), 170.

3. Although the colleges where we teach in upstate New York attract students from diverse backgrounds, including Native American students from the local Mohawk reservation, classes tend to be made up primarily of non-Native students who are generally unfamiliar with Native culture and literature. This particular population of students presents its own unique challenges, which we address in this essay, and, understandably, results from teaching a predominantly Native (or Haudenosaunee) student population would differ significantly.

4. Kenny, *Tortured Skins and Other Fictions*, 52.

5. Kenny, 66.

6. Ibid., 50.

7. Ibid., 120.

8. Ibid., 121.

9. Kenny, 100.

10. Kenny, 109.

11. Ibid.

12. Kenny, "Angry Rain: A Brief Autobiographical Memoir from Boyhood to College," *Contemporary Authors Autobiography Series* 22 (1995): 121–172.

13. Kenny, *Carving Hawk: New & Selected Poems* (Buffalo, NY: White Pine Press, 2002), 344.

14. Paula Gunn Allen, "A Stranger in my Own Life," *ASAIL Newsletter* 3 (Winter, 1979), http://oncampus.richmond.edu/faculty/ASAIL/SAILns/31.html> (7 September 2007.

15. (Maurice Kenny, *Angry Rain (Contemporary Authors Autobiography Series*, 1995), 129.

16. (Kenny, *Carving Hawk 344)*.

EIGHT

THE SPIRIT OF INDEPENDENCE

Maurice Kenny's Tekonwatonti / Molly Brant: Poems of War

Craig S. Womack

Looking back at this essay, written in 1994, it represents an audacity I no longer possess since I probably would no longer attempt publishing on Iroquois writing, a subject I know little about (with the exception of recent work on Pauline Johnson's prose style which I hope maintains a maximum reserve in terms of trying to assert anything about its Iroquoian underpinnings). Still the piece marks a point in time when, urged on by my faith in the powers of formalism, the ability of texts to reveal themselves, the value of thematic treatments, and a minimal amount of historical or cultural commitment that might solidify the revelation, I felt emboldened to try my hand at most anything. I hesitated to re-publish it, but I hope that the inclusion of other writers who study Kenny from a much more solid foundation will strengthen what I took up sixteen years ago. One thing has not changed over the years, my admiration for the author's poems and this particular book that brings Molly Brant to life.

Citizens of the Six Nations have long been known as keepers of tribal histories. The Tuscaroran Reverend David Cusick probably wrote the first Native tribal history, *Sketches of Ancient History of the Six Nations*, published in 1848. Cusick "turned back to the blanket" after becoming disillusioned with Christianity, as did the Huron convert Peter Dooyentate Clarke, a missionary who later disappeared after writing *The Origins and Traditional History of the Wyandots* in 1870. Other examples include Tuscaroran chief Elias Johnson's 1881 *Legends, Traditions, and Laws of the Iroquois* and Arthur Parker's many works. The famous wampum belts, which served as mnemonic devices to help pass on cultural, historical, and ritual information by word of mouth, predated these written accounts.

Contemporary poet Maurice Kenny's unique combination of historic and poetic faculties is an excellent addition to this body of tribal histories as well as to American poetry in general. The author's work, a twelve-year effort, is an example of incarnation: Kenny gives historical data a voice, a personality, a spirit. He demonstrates that what one can imagine is as real, as vital, as important as written history. The poet, through his creative vision, speaks to the silence of American history, which has reduced powerful women like Molly Brant, wife of Sir William Johnson and leader of forces against the Americans in the Revolution, to mere footnotes.

Kenny's poetry employs themes that also are used by other contemporary Native American writers. These themes include survival in a culture that has already declared Native people vanished; the role of the past in creating the present; cultural decay and the shallowness of contemporary values; a universe infused with spirit that can guide and instruct those willing to listen; the ongoing presence of ancestors; and the reverence of language. As the narrator E. Pauline Johnson says in Kenny's poem "Generations," "My poems drum as a partridge drums on the earth; / they do not sing in falsetto."[1] The same can be said of Kenny, whose poems do not name the literati or contain pretentious literary allusions. Instead, he draws from the earth as text; the landscape and the natural world are the poetic tradition out of which he writes. Additionally, he draws from Iroquoian culture and history as well as both European written poetic forms and the oral tradition. In this he is consistent with many other contemporary Native American poets.

Kenny has written poems inspired by traditional chant and dances, influenced by what one critic calls "moments of intersection"[2] with nature and the past; his travels have inspired poems in which he recreates the spirit of place. As Andrew Wiget observed, "Kenny sings of connections with the land and history, delighting in the smallest moments of being, which disclose in their sudden beauty and grace the oneness of all living things."[3] His poems also deal with displacement and the difficulties incurred in returning home and creating home when separated from one's familiar landscape. Against such discomforting problems, however, Kenny invokes a continuous ceremonial naming of sacred elements of landscape. This naming demonstrates the possibility of living in relationship to the soil even when away from home, the potential for bringing home into exile through participation in nature. These feelings for the environment are not a mere romantic subjectivity. Carolyn D. Scott says, "The recurrence of these images produces not the tiresome pretentiousness of private feeling, but rather intimations one can recognize as those belonging to home—the village fires."[4] In other words, the response to nature has specific ceremonial precedents among Kenny's people, the Iroquois.

What makes *Molly Brant: Poems of War* different from other historical accounts is that the author writes the poems from an insider's viewpoint. The poems provide an immersion in the past as complete as what James Welch accomplishes in *Fools Crow*. This recovery of traditional life differs somewhat from the aforementioned novel, however, in that Kenny keeps the past continually linked to the present and draws attention to Molly Brant's ongoing influence. Native authors have shown in their writing a sacred respect for ancestral voices; they have provided many portrayals of these formative influences and have discussed means in which they still speak; Kenny, however, has created a full cultural context for a historical figure. This work surpasses Kenny's earlier book *Blackrobe: Isaac Jogues* because of the depth he has achieved in presenting Molly's consciousness, personality, and philosophy. In addition to the portrayal of Molly Brant, the author gives voice to a number of other complex characters.

Kenny begins his history in a traditional manner, with an evocation of the sacred. Rather than beginning with Molly's birth, Kenny reaches back to legendary time, to earlier beginnings, as a traditional storyteller would. I use the terms *legendary* and *legend* because the author has expressed, in writing and in conversations, his preference for those words over *mythical* and *myth*. Kenny argues that stories have ongoing relevance and feels that the former terms express that sense better than the latter.

The poem "Te-Non-An-At-Che" names the elements of creation in order to show that all things begin with stories:

> Water was first
> Morning rolled
> fog steamed
> from mud
> where pollywogs
> wiggled.
> And legends began
> drop
> drop[5]

Kenny links legends, dripping down through time, with water, the first element. Stories and creation occur simultaneously. A traditional oral historical sequence occurs in the poem. This progression begins with naming primordial elements, naming plants and animals, naming persons, naming the people's migration as they journey forth from the place of origin.

Kenny is a poet of concrete images, of vivid characterization, of realistic voices. When he employs symbols—blood and strawberries, for example—these work as recurring motifs that resonate with meaning because they have a place in the stories of his people, and they have a cumulative effect as they pile on meaning throughout the corpus of his work. Kenny is not an obscure symbolist. He believes in poetry as an oracular performance as much as a written form. Those who have heard him read know that, for him, poetry means movement, physicality, sound; the release of adrenaline and the pounding of the bloodstream. Kenny's poetry has a performative quality. For instance, one succinct poem, written in the French Jesuit Abbé Picquet's voice, simply reads, "Ah! / Behold / my dream."[6] Picquet makes this proclamation as he gazes at the military fort he coerced Mohawk men into building. During an oral performance of this line, the listener witnesses Kenny becoming Abbé Picquet.

Kenny's presentation of poetry is consistent with oral cultures in which the storyteller becomes the story. Spoken words are, by definition, actions, not arbitrary symbols; thus, word and deed are closely related. This is the way stories can be passed on and remembered in the absence of written backups—by total emotional involvement of both teller and listener. Stories, then, are a re-experiencing of events. They come to pass in their tellings. The storyteller uses gesture, movement, voice modulation, sophisticated imitations of characters, and other techniques that all reduce the objective distance between listener, teller, and story. A complete identification between word and audience occurs. Kenny's use of repetition and parallelism gives his poems the rhythm of chant; and the purpose of chant, in oral cultures, is to aid listeners in remembering information passed down by word of mouth. Chant also has the larger spiritual purpose of creating being through language so that whatever is spoken of comes to pass. Kenny's poems convey an oral quality in another way—through the author's re-creation of the voices of Chief Hendrick, Aliquippa, Chief Cornplanter, and others. Through these Iroquoian voices, Kenny captures the superlative oratory for which his people are known.

Kenny makes the historical treatment of Molly Brant and other characters particularly interesting by creating an imaginative dialogue between historical accounts and poetic voices. For example, in an excerpt from a historical text, Kenny records James Thomas Flexner, an American historian and biographer of Sir William Johnson and George Washington. Flexner comments on Molly Brant's capacity for violence.[7] On the following page, Molly specifically addresses the accusation herself and denies it, stating that she loathes war and will accept it only as the last alternative for survival. She says, "I hate war, but love this earth and my kin more / than I hate battles and bravery. This / is my passion . . . to survive with all around me."[8]

For a poet who makes repeated claims not to be a storyteller, Kenny has demonstrated a strong narrative voice. Recently, he has experimented with short stories in *Rain and Other Fictions*; in the preface to that book, he says,

> Never have I seriously considered myself a storyteller. . . . I have always proclaimed that I am a singer of poetic song, and that my betters in fiction—Simon J. Ortiz, Peter Blue Cloud, Leslie Silko, Elizabeth Cook-Lynn—can out-spin me for tales. I have, however, occasionally pursued narrative in both story and one-act plays, not necessarily to spin a tale but more to delineate character. Narrative is a challenge. For me, it is a morning exercise as well, an exercise in ridding poetry of the statement of prose. . . . The stories and one-act play in this book make a small bundle, and my clutch of narrative poems would make a smaller bundle, still.[9]

Yet Kenny's strongest previous works are *Blackrobe: Isaac Jogues* (1982) and *The Mama Poems* (1984). The former was nominated for a Pulitzer Prize, the latter received the American Book Award. Both books focus on single persons—an ambitious and lascivious Jesuit missionary in the first case and the author's mother in the second. Both are books of narrative poems. In *Molly Brant: Poems of War*, the storytelling voice that the poet has been insecure about has risen to new heights of power.

The genius of the book is that Kenny creates voices that are lyrical and, at the same time, convincing as speech. A good example is the character of George Crohan, an Irish immigrant, an important influence in the Mohawk Valley. The poet captures the feeling of Croghan's concerns as settler, trader, and farmer, and represents them with a voice at once colloquial and poetic:

> Unsung and I don't give a damn. Not medaled, and I don't give a fart. No recompense, no spoils, no vast acreage for valor, and I don't give a damn fart for that either. I'm a woodsman. A father. A friend. I till the soil, I arrow a bird, I shoot a deer.[10]

In this book, Kenny demonstrates more than ever that he has an ear for American speech and can create a wide range of voices. Examples of this diversity appear in the poems about Jennie, a Black slave held by William Johnson, and her daughter Juba. When the reader encounters Juba for the first time, she is repeating something that sounds like a ceremonial incantation concerning fire, and one wonders if Juba is practicing some kind of voodoo:

> jumm jumm jumm jumm
> fire jump fire jump
> sprinkle beads onto these flames
> jumm jumm jumm jumm.[11]

Juba continues by chanting a spell-like incantation, and a lively scene is created of a girl ritualistically feeding a fire. In a later poem spoken in Jennie's voice, Kenny reveals that Juba is mentally unstable and that her father is William Johnson:

> Some say Juba is his chile. Now.
> She ain't right in the head. She jumm-jumms
> most of the time. Now.
> He don't come back anymore. I ain't no chile no more.[12]

Kenny captures a broad linguistic diversity in these poetic voices—Iroquoian orators, slaves, immigrants, French Jesuit missionaries, Mohawk women, as well as more contemporary figures such as Mohawk poet E. Pauline Johnson. He structures the book in such a way—as he did *Blackrobe: Isaac Jogues*—that multiple voices comment on the same person, and the characters are examined from many different angles. As with Juba, he reveals characters cumulatively, and their personalities fall together for the reader as the book progresses.

The center of attention, and an omnipresence in all poems, is Molly herself. Through his creative act, the author has established a strong relationship between himself and Molly Brant, evident because the poems are so convincingly and lovingly rendered. This makes the book an interesting addition to the poet's corpus, since the Jogues poems reflect a certain enmity toward the central character, whom Kenny depicts as the culture slayer.

An important consideration in evaluating Molly's personality and actions is the fact that she frames her identity within the context of an oral and communal culture rather than as a lone individual. In the poem, "I, Tekonwatonti," Molly's actions, especially with regard to warfare, are predicated on the effect they will have on her community rather than on political loyalties to the British, French, or Americans:

> I,
> I,
> Tekonwatonti, I
> no, we.[13]

In switching from *I* to *we*, Molly subjugates her individual needs to the needs of the community.

Another poem that reflects this communal identity is "Prayer for Aroniateka / Hendrick," an expression of mourning as well as thanksgiving, based on the Mohawk Condolence Prayer. Those who are grieving at the death of a longhouse chief offer this prayer to ease their sorrow. Kenny's poem, a prayer for Hendrick after his death in the battle of Lake George in 1755, shows that an individual death is a group concern. The narrator of the poem is the communal *we*, the voice of the community, which calls on a powerful assemblage of ancestral voices to honor and aid Hendrick:

> We come with his father and his father and his father
> father and his father and his father
> father and his father and his father
> father and his father and his father
> father and his father and his father
> until the memory no longer contains his father
> father and his father and his father
> to the morning sky woman fell
> with birds from the highest sky
> to the turtle's back
> and brought his father and his cousin
> the twins of the sky.[14]

Molly recognizes that her very survival depends on sticking to her blood, adhering to communal ties. After William's death, when she and their eight children are turned out of Johnson Hall, she says,

> We'll contend. Take less, perhaps.
> We won't starve. A roof
> remains over our heads.
> We stand in a circle.[15]

Molly's tendency to see herself as *we* rather than *I* provides an important context for her becoming a woman warrior after she learns of George Washington's vow to wipe the Mohawk off the face of the earth. As a clan mother responsible for the safety of the community, Molly regards the danger to her people as a personal threat.

"I, Tekonwatonti" is the first of seven consecutive poems that give voice to Molly's memorable personality. The sequence of seven poems is significant, of course, because of the sacredness of the number seven in relation to the cardinal directions and the realms of earth, sky, and water.

The poem "Picking Gooseberries" places Molly in a legendary context of multiple voices in dialogue, arranged on the page like the text for a play. Molly converses with Blue Bird, Black Bird, and Red Bird about women's concerns and, more specifically, about William's demands. It is the talk of women at ease among themselves, out of earshot of men. In his poems and in conversations, Maurice Kenny often has depicted berry-picking as an important time for socialization, gossip, jokes, and storytelling, and "Picking Gooseberries" is a wonderful addition to that association. Berries, especially strawberries, are central images for the poet: In Iroquois storytelling, the Little People who lived in a quarry without meat, took in Ragged Boy, who shared game with them. They, in turn, gave him the gift of strawberries and stories to take back to the people. When he returned to his community, he found that his people had moved and were starving, and the strawberries and stories restored them to health.[16]

Throughout the body of his work, Kenny associates berry-picking with blood—from the pricked fingers of the pickers. In "What the Chroniclers Did Not Record," the narrator says of Molly, "[S]he gathered summer berries, stained cheeks / with their blood. . . ."[17] Of Doris in *The Mama Poems*, the speaker recalls,

> Girls were raised
> To work, to carry water for the laundry, wash dishes, scrub floors,
> Shake the tick in the morning wind, scythe the grasses, and
> bend, bend,
> Forever bend in the berry fields where you bled profusely on
> the fruit.
> Your face and gingham spotted with your first knowledge, your first
> Lesson. You were never able to wash the blood away. It stuck, hard
> And dark to your cheek, your hands. . . .[18]

By associating Molly with berry-picking, Kenny links her to the contemporary women of power who recur throughout his poetry. The omnipresent blood imagery creates a simultaneity of past, present, and future. Blood, in the sense of bloodline, connects ancestors with those in the present, as well as those to come. A major theme in the book, which comes to the foreground in the last two sections, "Women / Memory" and "Epilogue," is Molly's continuing existence, in the landscape and in her contemporary progeny. In the poem "Generations," E. Pauline Johnson contrasts William's diminishment and Molly's continuance. She proclaims Molly to have the stronger life, which lasts and continues to speak to people. She associates both Molly and William with blood: Molly in a positive way, because her blood is connected to the earth; William negatively, because his blood is associated with growing smaller:

> If I open a vein, I shall fill this hanky with valley earth
> Molly brought to Canada, dragging
> Her children along by the hairs on their heads,
> Not with his bones and blood that she left (against her will)

In that shallow grave near the river.
He's only a dab of blood on this hanky.[19]

The claim that Johnson's blood has minimal influence is a damning statement, coming from a traditional culture that reckons kinship back many generations. The very last poem in the book, "Old Coyote in the Adirondacks," contrasts William's waning power with Molly's continuing influence today, even on nonhumans. The poem describes a coyote singing "on the curve / of his hill." It does not say what song the coyote sings as it "enter[s] / the night," but the poem's silence is suggestive.[20] Its placement at the end of the volume strongly implies that it is Molly's song the coyote sings. The penultimate poem in the collection backs up this assertion. In the midst of the cultural loss, destructive technologies, and waste depicted in "Sitting in the Waters of Grasse River," the creative elements that survive, such as Coyote, such as E. Pauline Johnson, such as Maúrice Kenny, continue to sing Molly's song.[21] This perpetual song in the natural world counterbalances the obliteration of native women's voices from written American history. The poem entitled "Beth Brant, 1981: Letter & Post Card"[22] establishes a relationship between women warriors, who use words.[23] The poems move back and forth between past and present, and Molly's life dramatizes the fact that responsibility for language precedes action; thus contemporary native writers using language for survival have an affinity with warriors from the past, who spoke and fought. Beth Brant, the contemporary Mohawk poet and fiction writer mentioned in the title of the poem, is a blood descendant of Molly.

Kenny depicts Molly as a woman in a community of women with strong voices; in Iroquoian culture, women have powerful positions in the longhouse and a strong influence on the political and social life of the nation. In her book, *The Iroquois in the American Revolution*, Barbara Graymont states,

> The practice of matrilineal descent gave women a unique position. Each clan was entitled to a certain number of chiefs, and the matrons of the clans could appoint and depose these chiefs. The white wampum belts which indicated the hereditary names of the chiefs were kept by the women. When a chief died, he did not pass his title on to his son, for titles were hereditary only in the clan; the son belonged to his mother's, not his father's clan. The chief's title would be inherited by one of his brothers or one of his sister's sons, or another male member of his clan matron's lineage.
>
> The mothers also had much influence with the warriors. During the American Revolution, Mary Brant [another name for Molly], Mohawk widow of Sir William Johnson and herself a clan mother,

> was able to sway the wavering warriors and keep them loyal to the British. The women, usually through a warrior chosen as their speaker, could always make their wishes known in council. Even an esteemed white woman living in Indian country could exercise unusual prerogatives, as did the Tory Sarah McGinnis when she prevented a wampum belt bearing news of an American victory over the British from going farther than her village. When the council could not agree on a certain issue, they referred the problem to the council of the clan mothers. Among the Iroquois, the women thus had greater status and more control over the affairs of their nation than did the women of the European countries and their colonial settlements.[24]

In Kenny's poems, Molly's boldness, her flouting of English tradition in her marriage to William, and her prodigious ability to learn White culture while remaining quintessentially Mohawk make her a singular personality. George Crohan, an Irish immigrant who became influential among the Iroquois, says of Molly in one poem,

> She knew how to hoe and how to sew.
> She could command servants and an army.
> She could birth a child and scalp a Frenchman.
> She could dine the governor and hunt mud frogs
> Or snap a turtle's neck before presenting his soup.
> Nothing was beyond her accomplishment, her reach.[25]

Molly's gentility and beauty are offset by a savvy . . . refusal to be possessed like the white women of William's class. Despite her access to White culture, she maintains a strong relationship with the earth and a spirit-based view of the universe. She combines the two cultures in creative and powerful ways. In "Flight," a poem about her exile after the American Revolution, Molly says, "I left my son's placenta in leaves / tied with wild grapevines."[26] This description of the return of life-giving tissue from Molly's own body to the soil strongly dramatizes her relationship with the earth. In the same poem, Molly goes on to say:

> I carried a small packet of soil,
> earth rich and dark in claim,
> moist from women's sweat working fields of squash,
> still firm from feet dancing in celebration,
> warm with William's footprint,

vibrant with Hendrick's oratory.
I fled.[27]

The passage shows Molly's recognition of the power of the earth to absorb human activity and to carry spirit voices. She carries a packet of earth to a new place, in a poignant attempt to bring home into her place of exile, to carry with her that which forms her, the most fundamental part of her identity. Molly's pain results from leaving behind part of herself in the landscape, the place where her kin and her ancestors lie buried. Kenny closely ties the soil to memory and culture: "A people who do not remember: / *rain which falls upon a rock.*"[28] Rain that falls on a rock does not penetrate the soil; forgetting one's culture involves forgetting the place from which one comes, the soil beneath one's feet. The clan mother Aliquippa says,

Memory
Does not die under autumn leaves, crisp and brown;
Memory is on the wind, the shine of stars,
The echo of song and story told winter nights.[29]

Kenny brings out Molly's natural acceptance of inexplicable phenomenoa and mystery in the poem "The Lights Are Always Near."[30] Here Molly lovingly explains that no one needs to fear the supernatural. The English mistake Molly's traditionalism for witchcraft, and they blame her for all the problems in the colonies: barrenness, drought, and war. Her husband William, however, recognizes that natural elements, not witchcraft, define Molly:

Yes, I laugh.
True, you are a witch, alchemist
Of September apples, red and savory
In the bin of the springhouse;
You are the bite of cider,
The bitter of bush cranberries,
The smart of fire rising under
Your kitchen kettles. . . .[31]

This continues Kenny's custom of fusing characters so closely with the natural environment that there is no separation between their physical bodies and the elements of nature. Previous poems such as "Mulleins Are My Arms" and "Legacy" have emphasized the internalization of nature within the body of the speaker. This breaks down the division under which Western thought has labored for so long—the difference between an internal view and an external view of the physical world, the opposition of flesh and spirit. The fluidity of Maurice Kenny's work makes it seem natural for a human to speak for rocks and trees and water, because humans are composed of such elements themselves.

The poems also can be viewed as war literature because they show the effects of war, not only on warriors but on a culture, on the landscape, on creation, on all one's relations. Molly fights against the extermination promised by George Washington. Barbara Graymont says,

The expedition against the Six Nations would be one of the most carefully planned campaigns of the entire war. General Washington, fully aware of the significance of the Indian-Tory devastations on the frontier, wanted to remove the menace once and for all. . . . A strike against the Indians would humble them and perhaps cause them to ask for peace. Total destruction of their villages and crops, even if it did not pacify them, would make them a greater burden to the British and divert foodstuffs required by the British army to the support of the Indians.[32]

Graymont points out that the Iroquois did not have the luxury of remaining neutral during the war. She writes that "for over a century [prior to the Revolution] the Iroquois had been accustomed to thinking of the English as one people—the children of the Great King beyond the sea."[33] No matter who they sided with, the Iroquois would face repercussions, and "because of both historic economic dependence and geographic contiguity, they could not withdraw completely, ignoring the whites and their quarrel."[34] Graymont has documented that the Colonists often employed barbarous methods of warfare. She reports that American troops led by Colonel Goose Van Schaick lay waste to an entire Onondaga village, killing twelve and taking thirty-three prisoners, most of them women surprised in a cornfield. The Onondaga reported that the soldiers raped the women despite General James Clinton's earlier written warning: "Bad as the savages are, they never violate the chastity of any women, their prisoners. Although I have very little apprehension that any of the soldiers will so far forget their character as to attempt such a crime on the Indian women who may fall into their hands, yet it will be well to take measures to prevent such a stain upon our army."[35]

Molly understands the unavoidable connection between war and loss, no matter what the justification:

wolf
clan
  paints red
    for war
  paints black
    for mourning[36]

A loss is incurred the moment the decision is made to go to war, requiring ceremonial recognition of grief even before the first bodies fall. Even though Molly aligns her warriors with the British, she feels no great loyalty to their cause. She recognizes that the political power brokers do the talking, while the young men and their families do the bleeding: "The rebels will win, and we lose, / not the redcoats; we, we the people, / the 'real people' will lose."[37] The phrase *we the people* is ironic in that, in the U.S. Constitution, these same words exclude the Native peoples who predated the loyalists and Colonists. During the Revolution, these "real people" are the true losers, and their fight, against biological and cultural extinction, has much higher stakes.

As a leader, Molly accepts responsibility for the death of her warriors: "In death their blood / will scar my hands forever," and "the loss will be too great / to bear."[38] She must avoid unnecessary waste of life, while at the same time protecting and insuring the survival of her people and culture. Thus, she prays,

> Give me good sense
> so I may not waste
> a single drop of blood
> of these young and brave
> who fight for England now
> but truly for the survival
> and strength of the Longhouse.[39]

In a poem entitled "Molly: Passions," Molly summarizes her philosophy of war. She particularizes her viewpoint by first naming those elements of creation that make life worth living: "Yes, oh yes, passions for blackberry / blossoms, the clank of deer bones winning games, / river water sluicing against canoes . . ."[40] Molly will accept war only if it is the sole alternative to seeing her relatives wiped off the face of the earth: "I hate war, but love this earth and my kin more / than I hate battles and bravery. This / is my passion . . . to survive with all around me." She fights for the very thing that has created Mohawk people: the land, which contains their stories and their dreaming of themselves, "for a long march to defend our priceless birthright / to new dawns and darknesses, our old stories / and old songs."[41] Finally, Molly fights not only for humans but for the spirit and substance of the land and the creatures that occupy the land, against their potential destroyers:

> Who would not
> ". . . defend her mother's womb."
> All around me is my mother's womb.

I lay claim to it.
This is my passion: life. And the right
to all it holds: blackberry blossoms,
marsh iris, the growl of bear at night,
light rising and falling upon our lodges,
the rivers that bathe us and slack our thirst
and that old plum tree flowering winter with snow.[42]

Sir William Johnson, an Irish immigrant to the colonies who was appointed superintendent of Iroquois affairs in 1746 and who enlisted Mohawk warriors on the British side against the French, married Molly in a tribal ceremony but not according to British law. In the poem entitled "Sir William Johnson: His Daily Journal," William explains that he falls philosophically between George Crohan, who believeed in land acquisition through forceful moderation, and George Washington, who supported total extermination of those who occupied the land. William feels sympathy for the Mohawk because he has Mohawk sons and thus a vested interest in the people's survival. However, he does not become a member of their community, and he posits value in his individual ownership of parts of the Mohawk Valley. William acts like a traditional only in order to gain advantages in trade. He displays genuine affection for Molly, but he does not love her enough to allow her to get in the way of land acquisition. In keeping with the incipient agrarian tradition of his time, William sees no value in the wilderness until it is turned under by the plow:

Truly, do I thirst, tremble at the sight
of unclaimed woods, woods which do not echo
the sounds of an ax striking bark;
earth unplowed, seedless, a womb virgin
having borne neither phallic plow nor fruit.[43]

This avowal of the virtues of a tamed landscape extends to his view of women. Just as William advocates penetration of the soil, he also values women in direct relationship to their fruitfulness:

Ahhhhh! Woman, I'll round they belly to a hundred sons.
Woman and land: the earth is a fallow woman,
its portals dark and mysterious, yielding the zenith
in stratospheric music which men only hear
when eyes are closed, chest and thighs sticky
in lustful sweat, mucilaged to the fat of her

scented flesh, writhing in groans, tendering
her to orgasm. . . .[44]

William comes across as a buffoon in this poem, and Kenny's hilarious performance of the piece with a macho Falstaffian bravado is highly memorable. Women and earth, according to William, do not have a fundamental integrity of their own apart from their usefulness to man. William seems both excited and threatened by Molly's power, a power not atypical for an Iroquoian woman but anathema from a British standpoint. He misinterprets Molly's abilities as an overbearing masculinity:

Molly, I nearly said
Man like man: Cut my tongue, couple my hands
To be the step for your boot to mount the black gelding,
To ride off, possibly to die as I would die
For these acres of woods and field, for this flag
The crown.[45]

The strong castration image, suggested by the black gelding and by William as bootstep for Molly's mounting, implies that William fears this woman can entertain aristocracy *and* lead warriors, yet he seems titillated by her manly qualities as well.

Although Molly plays a warrior's role, Kenny gives no indication that she has a warrior's spirit or a masculine sexual identity. In many cases in traditional cultures, a man or woman who had a homosexual orientation would have a matching social role that the tribe nurtured, accepted, and considered a part of the person's spiritual identity. The community saw such persons as powerful individuals who should be treated respectfully. Although Kenny was the first Native author to publish an essay on the role of the berdarche—he was concerned that much of this information had been purposefully hidden by white anthropologists—he gives no indication that Molly is one of these Two-Spirited women (a person who can see from both the male and female worlds.) Molly's warrior role seems to be borne strictly out of necessity. She states that she loathes war, and, if not for the threat of imminent extermination, she would have nothing to do with it. Additionally, in Iroquoian culture, it was a norm for women to be closely involved in warrior activities. Graymont cites several instances of other Iroquoian women in battle; of the influence of women on warriors, she says,

The women had significant influence with the warriors and could frequently make or break a war party by their support or disapproval

> of the warriors' enterprise. It was the women who provided the warriors with moccasins and charred corn pounded into meal and sweetened with maple sugar for their journey. The women also had the power to veto a war declaration by withholding these supplies.[46]

Furthermore, Molly's natural proclivities do not seem inclined toward a masculine role. In fact, Molly's natural femininity makes her male role as a warrior all the more striking. The Seneca clan mother Aliquippa explains women's reasons for involvement in the French and Indian War:

> Women warriors. We assumed we fought
> for freedom, our land, earth, for the joy
> of dawn and the rest of dark night.
> We were told the French would burn
> our villages, decimate our children,
> mutilate the prowess of our men.[47]

Aliquippa goes on to say that women, as clan leaders, maintain serious responsibilities for leading men and instructing them in communal maintenance:

> Were we
> not the leaders of our clans, obliged to prod
> the men to hunt or war to feed and protect
> the village our hands constructed, our wombs
> populated, our minds furbished?[48]

Thus, powerful women like Molly and Aliquippa, responsible for the welfare of the community, must defend it, if necessary.

In many interesting ways, both William and Molly resemble characters in earlier works like *Blackrobe* and *The Mama Poems*. Kenny depicts the two male figures, William Brant and Isaac Jogues, as being out of balance in terms of their sexual appetites. Jogues is attracted to the boys in the Mohawk village where he proselytizes. The poems show him casting furtive glances at the young men. This, in and of itself, would not create a problem in traditional Mohawk culture, which, generally speaking, accepted sexual variance with much more tolerance than contemporary society does. However, Jogues, an outsider in every sense of the word, loathes the traditional ways of the people and spouts words of Christian damnation in response to Mohawk sexual practices. The poem "Hoantteniate"[49] implicitly suggests that Jogues is involved sexually with his adopted Mohawk brother (at least, this reader interprets the poem that way). The poem shows a softer, more loving side of Jogues, but when he sees the same expression of sexuality among the people, he finds it abominable.

In the *Molly Brant* poems, Kenny depicted William's relationships with women as equally unbalanced. George Croghan says of him,

> He was profligate, Will was, and she courted
> his desires salaciously. She was young and ripe,
> ripe as the yellow pear hanging on his front yard tree.
> She was young, she was full of ginger, mustard;
> Will was lecherous, a woman masher, taken too early
> from his mother's own teat. . . .[50]

William's lust takes the form of relationships with his slaves and myriad other women and includes bigamy. William purchased Catherine Weisenberg as an indentured servant from a Mohawk Valley farmer. The author states in the prologue that William, in blatant denial of his tribal marriage to Molly, "married Catherine the night she died and legitimized their union and children. Kenny indicates that "certain historians have hinted that Johnson may have fathered some two-hundred children, including Juba [a slave], by various women."[51]

Furthermore, a similarity exists in the tension between Sir William and Molly in this book and between Doris and Andrew in *The Mama Poems*. In both cases, adoring women devote themselves to men who behave sometimes lovingly and sometimes scandalously and rapaciously. Just as William is profligate and views women as valuable only in their usefulness to men, Andrew can also be cruel:

> No doubt he gave you a rough time,
> probably whacked you once or twice.
>
> .
> .
> .
>
> and I've heard it said he'd pinch
> a waitress' buttocks, never refused a bed.
> He taught you how to drive a car
> and promptly took the Ford away.
> He'd buy you a new dress and grumbled
> if you wore it. He even upbraided you
> for buying a pound of butter
> at fifteen cents a pound.[52]

Andrew, like Jogues and William, seems to take advantage of the women in his life. (Jogues unfeelingly used Wolf Mother, the Mohawk woman who adopted him.) However, Andrew has qualities the speaker admires. In the context of the poems and in interviews, the author has described how his father provided a link to Mohawk culture and, in fact, rescued him in his teenage years when he got into trouble and risked being sent to a reformatory. It is difficult not to apply these autobiographical statements to *The Mama Poems* because the author himself has chosen to begin the collection with a biographical statement about his mother. In the poems, Kenny states that the last word from Andrew's mouth is "Doris" and that he carries a snapshot of her until his death.[53] So the male–female relationships in *Molly* and *The Mama Poems* involve a kind of love that stings yet endures, that remains healthy in some ways and disturbing in others.

Kenny presents the tension between William and Molly in a scene that is both taut and playful. William is seated before her. Knife in hand, she plucks his hair for battle:

> No, no,
> I won't take too much,
> my knife is sharp.
> You don't trust my knife?
> I wouldn't hank it from your scalp.[54]

These relationships that grind against one another seem to have a kind of passion and vitality caused by the very elements that make them disturbing. If nothing else, each partner is so memorable to the other that they carry each other's spirit with them to the grave.

In *The Mama Poems*, Doris, like Molly, has prodigious talents and can transcend male–female roles:

> Your qualities were never baking,
> but when you rolled up the sleeves
> and baited your own hook,
> or cleaned a mess of trout
> or string of November rabbits
> even when we demanded you darn
> socks or heal blisters, fight
> a cold. . . .[55]

The Mama Poems end, as do the *Molly Brant* poems, with the speaker's realization that the lives of powerful women transcend death through their ongoing presence in the land:

> I believe in echoes now,
> in the earth that holds you. I believe in a bird,
> its flight, though I'm not sure which one, hawk
> or seagull; the cedar near your grave, and the lake
> not far away that you feared from childhood.[56]

It seems, then, that Kenny brings vitality to his presentation of characters by drawing on relationships that are familiar to him and infusing this personal background into his poetry. The overall effect is compelling; what is particularly interesting is that it fits a larger cultural tension. The author begins *The Mama Poems* with the Mohawk version of the Iroquois creation story, which reports a strong male–female tension:

Right-handed Twin came naturally from his mother, the daughter impregnated by the West Wind, of Sky-woman. But his brother, Left-handed Twin, impatiently sprang early from his mother's armpit and killed her from his unnatural escape from her body.[57]

The matricide in the legendary story comes up in an interesting way in "On the Staten Island Ferry," from *The Mama Poems*:

> You brought me here when I was ten
> . . .
> A friend suggested I write
> a novel of how I wanted to push
> you off the ferry into the wake . . .
> fall like Sky-woman fell form the old world.
> My friend said impatience cured
> curiosity, but I don't think novels
> cure pain not intention of guilt.
> This morning the sun hangs
> in the eastern sky and the moon
> sits in the west. They eye each other,
> jealous siblings never
> willing to share a dandelion
> nor rib of venison. As I could not do
> without a mother we cannot do
> without their argument.
> They'll continue contesting
> on such mornings as this, and I
> will continue pleased that you
> had not been swallowed in the ferry's wake.
> . . .
> My father took me home again.[58]

The poem begins with the line about the boy's mother bringing him to the ferry and ends with his father taking him home. In the midst of all this ambivalence, the poem alludes to the legend about Left-handed Twin accidentally killing his mother, and it seems to suggest that the story that informs the poem actually keeps things in balance: "As I could not do / without a mother we cannot do / without their argument." In fact, the legend seems to help the speaker deal with his feelings and provides a cathartic release for his hostilities. The analysis here is not an attempt to be psychoanalytical, but, because the author himself raises these issues in the poems, it makes for an interesting comparison. In the whole body of work, one sees this kind of tension often: Wolf Mother protecting Jogues against the leaders of the Bear Moiety, who want to kill him[59]; sibling, parental, and masculine and feminine tension in the poem "Sometimes . . . Injustice" in *The Mama Poems*[60]; Molly with the knife to Sir William's scalp in *Molly Brant*. If anything, because of their consistency in all three books and the way they hearken back to legendary stories, these themes strengthen the poetry and broaden the author's vision, depicting vital, passionate, sometimes disturbing relationships between men and women.

In addition to these interesting personal relationships, *Molly Brant* reminds us of those person who suffered under both banners—the Union Jack and the star-spangled one. The poems suggest that, in addition to honoring George Washington as father of our country, we must acknowledge other names for the first president if we wish to invoke the liberating power of truth. The Mohawk called him the "town exterminator" because of his policy of total annihilation. Cornplanter, in 1790, had this to say to George Washington: "When your army entered the country of the Six Nations, we called you Town Destroyer: and to this name when that name is heard our women look behind them and turn pale, and our children cling close to the necks of their mothers."[61]

Kenny's poetry demonstrates that, in order to understand historical figures like Washington, we need to know all their names. Contemporary people can heal the wrongs of the past only by creative empathy, not by "putting the past behind us." Cultural memory—accessible through the imagination and brought to life in this body of poems—rather than cultural amnesia provides our best hope for survival. Lying and covering up, not truth-telling, threaten democracy. Traditional cultures have great potential in contemporary society because of the power they attribute to the word as a force for change. Furthermore, the creation of new stories that take into account modern circumstances is as important as the maintenance of old ones. Traditions can be carried forward into the present by imagining, remembering, telling. Seneca clan mother Aliquippa prophesies,

Again
we will eat succotash, drink soup.
Singers will stand and sing, our daughters will
pick strawberries, wild and red, from the meadows.
Our men will thank the deer for his flesh.
Wolf will trot the old mountains
and the elders lead us in prayer.
We will have forgotten nothing.[62]

Kenny and Aliquippa have shown us a way of taking back our own history.

NOTES

1. Maurice Kenny, *Tekonwatonti/Molly Brant: Poems of War* (Fredonia, NY: White Pine Press, 1992), 181.
2. Michael Castro, foreword in Kenny, *Humorous And/Or Not So Humorous* (Buffalo: NY: Swift Kick, 1988.)
3. Andrew Wiget, *Native American Literature* (Boston, MA: Twayne Publishers, 1985), 112.
4. Carolyn D. Scott, "Baskets of Sweetgrass: Maurice Kenny's *Dancing Back Strong the Nation* and *I Am the Sun*," *Studies in American Indian Literatures* 7 (Winter 1983):10.
5. Kenny, *Tekonwatonti/Molly Brant*, 80.
6. Ibid., 41.
7. Ibid., 143.
8. Ibid., 145.
9. Kenny, *Rain and Other Fictions* (Fredonia, NY: White Pine Press, 1990), 9–10.
10. Kenny, *Tekonwatonti/Molly Brant*, 80.
11. Ibid., 88.
12. Ibid., 90.
13. Ibid., 62.
14. Ibid., 106.
15. Ibid., 125.
16. Kenny, *Between Two Rivers: Selected Poems 1956–1984* (Fredonia, NY: White Pine Press, 1987), 139.
17. Kenny, *Tekonwatonti/Molly Brant*, 168.
18. Kenny, *Between Two Rivers*, 137.
19. Kenny, *Tekonwatonti/Molly Brant*, 182.
20. Ibid., 196.
21. Ibid., 194–195.
22. Ibid., 52–53.

23. Ibid., 52–53.

24. Barbara Graymont, *The Iroquois in the American Revolution* (Syracuse, NY: Syracuse University Press, 1972), 13.

25. Kenny, *Tekonwatonti/Molly Brant*, 119.

26. Ibid., 157.

27. Ibid., 158.

28. Ibid., 130.

29. Ibid., 179.

30. Ibid., 69.

31. Ibid., 72.

32. Graymont, *The Iroquois in the American Revolution*, 193–194.

33. Ibid., 1.

34. Ibid., 1.

35. Ibid., 196.

36. Kenny, *Tekonwatonti/Molly Brant*, 135.

37. Ibid., 141.

38. Ibid., 146.

39. Ibid., 147.

40. Ibid., 144.

41. Ibid., 145.

42. Ibid., 145.

43. Ibid., 91.

44. Ibid., 92.

45. Ibid., 95–96.

46. Graymont, *The Iroquois in the American Revolution*, 21.

47. Kenny, *Tekonwatonti/Molly Brant*, 176.

48. Ibid., 177.

49. Kenny, *Between Two Rivers*, 130.

50. Kenny, *Tekonwatonti/Molly Brant*, 118.

51. Ibid., 202.

52. Kenny, *Between Two Rivers*, 144.

53. Ibid., 144.

54. Kenny, *Tekonwatonti/Molly Brant*, 101.

55. Kenny, *Between Two Rivers*, 145.

56. Ibid., 160.

57. Ibid., 135.

58. Ibid., 147.

59. Ibid., 117–123.

60. Ibid., 141.

61. Graymont, *The Iroquois in the American Revolution*, 192.

62. Kenny, *Tekonwatonti/Molly Brant*, 179.

NINE

PAINTING "WORD-PICTURES" IN PLACE

Maurice Kenny's Empathetic Imagination of Tekonwatonti / Molly Brant

Lisa Brooks

When I first set out to write a chapter that concerned Mohawk leader Joseph Brant, I was struck by a particular moment at Niagara, following the ravages of the Revolutionary War, when his sister Molly turned to a Mohican leader, traveling with his small entourage on a diplomatic mission, and essentially asked, "where are your women?" According to the Mohican leader, she said, "if these Indians were upon good business, they would certainly follow the customs of all nations—they would have some women with them, but now they have none."[1] Maurice Kenny raises a similar question in his own poetic portrait of *Tekonwatonti / Molly Brant*, inquiring why Native women leaders like Molly have been so "shockingly ignored by the historians." As he points out, although American culture is saturated with images of Indian "princesses" like Pocahontas, much less attention is paid to those full-fledged women who led in diplomacy and war. Before any article or book-length account had been published about Molly Brant, this Mohawk poet embarked on "nearly twelve years" of historical research and careful listening, piecing together the puzzles of Molly's life, and interpreting them through a Mohawk-specific framework.[2] In a 2005 interview, Chad Sweeney noted that Kenny considered *Tekonwatonti / Molly Brant, 1735–1795* to be "his most important work."[3] Creating evocative image-portraits in words, Kenny locates us firmly in a social and geographic Haudenosaunee (Iroquois) landscape, while drawing out intricate details and arresting insights with a poet's eye. When I wanted to understand more about Molly and her stance that day at Niagara, I turned to the work of Maurice Kenny.

CREATION: THE MOHAWK RIVER, "TE-NON-AN-AT-CHE"

From the first poems of this collection, Kenny's own intimate familiarity with the land of Molly's birth is evident. Kenny grew up in northern New York, sneaking into the back of his father's pickup truck on hunting trips, and gradually becoming, as he writes, "a hunter of words and images" as well as "song."[4] The book opens with an extended creation song, located in the flow of the Mohawk River, "Te-Non-An-At-Che." As he writes, "Water was first." Kenny begins his own creative effort with the origin of life, embracing simultaneous "legends" rooted in biological, geological, and cultural understandings of emergence:

Morning rolled
fog steamed
from mud
where pollywogs
wiggled.

And legends began
drop
drop[5]

Immediately, our eyes are drawn to the movement of water on the page, the aurality of this sound, to the activity of life emerging from within this richly saturated world. It is a world of stillness, in which motion is constant, signaling an awakening. It could be the first moment that life was created on this earth; it could be this morning, as the warming sun begins to break through, glistening on blades of grass. It could represent the emergence of life in the entire Mohawk River valley, or the poet's eye view of one warm, wet spring morning on a marsh, surrounded by blue flag and reeds.

Kenny's own experiential knowledge of the waterways and places of his ancestors profoundly informs his depiction of this space. From the use of specific toponyms to the naming of plants like blue flag (marsh iris) and pitcher plant, which are particular to the water saturated marshes and bogs of the northeast, the work is characterized by a tangible knowledge of place. In this opening poem, the water flows through a Mohawk-specific geography. From the first stanza, our eyes move with its course through a list of names, familiar only to those who know this river. First, the origin of its common name, the name of its people, demonstrating a linguistic evolution from Algonquian to Dutch to English: "Maguas, Mohaugs, Mohawks." Then, the naming of the rivers' tributaries, in a manner that reveals multiple layers of history:

Chuctanunda, Potash Creek, Burch
Briggs Run, Kayaderossearas, Sandsea Kill
drop
drop
drop
Schoharie, Otsquago, Alpaus, Stony
Garoga, Canajoharie, Sanquoit Flat.[6]

Followed by the naming of rivers to which the Mohawk is connected, by the water's flow, by trading routes, by the places which took in refugees from war, and by the author's own life experience: "Genesee, Black, Blue, St. Lawrence."[7]

These brooks and streams comprise the origins of the Mohawk, flowing from upland mountains and hills to join the river at various points along its course. Likewise, the names these tributaries have acquired reveal the peoples whose histories have merged with its own—the Mohawk place-names that persist (including Molly's home village of Canajoharie), as well as the Dutch, English, and French names that reflect aspects of its colonial history. Like tributaries, these histories all contribute to and become part of a multifaceted river; it contains them all. Yet, as Kenny styles it, reflecting the actual names of these tributaries in the present moment, the English names do not simply replace the Mohawk ones. The names tell the river's story, and importantly, they do not move in any clear sequential order—as some historians would have it, from Mohawk to Dutch to English to American—or along tributaries from west to east. Kenny does not impose a definitive order on the river or its history. Rather, he acknowledges that all of these strands are contributing to the constant flow and formation of the river, simultaneously.

These multiple strands are woven by the poet into a vast Indigenous tapestry. Following a long line of Haudenosaunee orators and authors, Kenny locates the life of his subject within a longstanding framework of Haudenosaunee historical narration, beginning with the water world of the Sky Woman story, the legends of "water creatures" and the birth of the "earth on turtle's back"; then moving through the coming of humans, "Algonquian" then "Haudenosaunee"; and culminating in the formation of the Great Law and the Longhouse. Only then does he allow in the bloodied landscape of colonial wars, which, like all other beings in this poem, emerge into an already extant world of the Mohawk River, building up on its banks. Molly's genealogy is similarly located in a long line of leadership that has coursed through this river: "Deganawidah Ayonwatha Hendrick Tekonwatonti."[8] She is a political descendant of the founders of the Great Law, as well as her clan chief, a prominent leader during the French and Indian wars. Her name emerges among the names of many leaders, Haudenosaunee, English, and American, in the midst of "War / War / and more War." Her name stands in for the many Native women omitted from the narrations of history, and Kenny demonstrates that she / they deserve equal standing among the names of famed leaders. Significantly, as figures such as Washington and Franklin do emerge, it is into the world of the Haudenosaunee and their Indigenous political traditions. It is only by coming through the Longhouse that they become American, even, ironically, as they foster war against their "founding fathers."

The images of fertile creation at the beginning of the poem are contrasted, and gradually overtaken, by images of this destructive force of "War" which produces "blood and guts and death." Importantly, Kenny acknowledges the Indigenous warfare that took place in the region long before the arrival of Europeans, when "Bones littered / open fields."[9] However, a later outbreak of warfare produces a time when "The river iced / and hearts chilled."[10] This ice age is not a natural outcome of the geology or ecology, but arises with the formation of Dutch and English villages on its banks, and ends with "the death of / Indians."[11] Twin stanzas, composed of lists of names, suggest an imposed chronology and a difference in spatial orientation. On the page, we see the formation of Haudenosaunee villages:

Andagaron Canajoharie Caughnawaga
Garoga Osseruenon Schandisse
Teonontogen

followed later by

Half Moon	Rotterdam	
Schnectady	Herkimer	Johnstown
German Flats	Rome	Fort Oriskany
Albany	Yonkers	New York City

The positioning of these names on the page suggests a contrasting geographical formation, with the Haudenosaunee villages appearing to flow along with the river, and in relation to each other, while the European villages exist as discreet entities in boxed rows (a contrast also reflected in Indigenous maps of the colonial period).[12] This spatial orientation also reflects the social and physical differences present within these villages, particularly in the way they plant. Consider the classic three sister's mound agriculture, depicted in the poem named for the multitribal village "At Ahquaga" (The Garden).[13] This companion plant "garden," cultivated by Haudenosaunee women, can accommodate any number of "edible plants" from "corn" and "beans" to "muskmelon / cabbage / turnips," in contrast to English gardens of monocrop rows, which remains the standard in American agriculture today. Towns like Oquaga flourished on Haudenosaunee waterways prior to the Revolution, as Indigenous people incorporated ancient traditions with newfound skills, tools, and crops. As Kenny suggests, it was colonial warfare that disrupted this process of adaptation, and allowed for this (often falsely naturalized) displacement of Iroquois villages, and in particular, the women's fields.

In this stanza, the "replacement narrative" of colonial historians, in which European towns "replace" Indian ones in a seemingly natural process, is starkly evident.[14] Following this list, an abrupt, transitory phrase stands apart in parentheses: "The Indian Lost." In one sense, this line suggests an ironic turn of phrase, mimicking the historians who dramatically misrepresented the end of Iroquois presence along the Mohawk, as well as the contemporary protesters of Haudenosaunee land claims who use this phrase in defense of their property rights. Yet, even as this proclamation is made, and these familiar colonial names replace those of the older villages, the river's tributaries enforce the memory of these places, maintaining their original names, and their original purpose, sustaining the Mohawk's identity as "TE-NON-AN-AT-CHE / (River flowing through mountains)" regardless of the changes on its banks. This suggests a dynamic of change and continuity that is constant in the Haudenosaunee landscape. Profound and violent changes take place here. Peoples, and entire villages, emerge, live, and die here, and yet the river itself holds forth the promise of renewal, of more change, and the sustenance of an identity that is rooted, quite firmly, in the seemingly never-moving mountains, and the continuous

drop
    drop
        drop
            drop

of the water's flow. This movement suggests that "The Indian Lost" is hardly the end of the story, as the telling by a contemporary Mohawk poet, living in his ancestors' territory, in dialogue with his relations, shows. Thousands of years of history, including the present moment, are thus contained in one poem, represented by the spiral of a river, which has a predictable course, but cannot be contained.

EMERGENCE: "MOLLY: PASSIONS"

Molly's own emergence, coming one fourth of the way into the book, is firmly located within the environment of the Mohawk River valley. The poem "Molly," which opens the section titled "Child / Woman," begins with this same watery place, each line starting with the "I" that "come[s] from" the "morning with light," the "river with song," "the marsh with reeds."[15] Yet, from this place of "muskrat, loon, raspberry, tamarack," "I, Tekonwatoniti" comes to recognize herself in a following poem among the progenitors of nations: "we women . . . my sisters in the fields of the sun / labor the birthing of generations."[16] Her birth is particularly honored as the emergence of a woman, who will birth more women, who comes from multiple strands of women, all of whom produce the clans of the nations. She recognizes that she is not only an "I," but "no, we," part of a body, descended of Sky Woman, who will "community the village / and populate our future."[17] Like those who came before her, and those will come from her; like every being who has emerged into this place, she will "break open membrane / and be counted" as "corn whispers the fields / as winds surge the dawn."

Rather than giving standard details of Molly's birth—where, when, by whom—Kenny has her gradually emerge into a densely inhabited space, coming to know herself in relation to a world that itself seems fecund, bursting with life, with the desire to live. Everything around her is animated, while her own voice seems amorphous, simultaneously asserting its individual desire to emerge, and reflecting the ebb and flow of the activity that surrounds it. She exists within the immediate environment, and within the layers of past and future generations of which the present is a part.

Importantly, even when William Johnson comes on the scene, he enters into Molly's space. In "Marriage Vow," the voice of Molly says, "I take you into my house."[18] Although later poems reveal that Molly becomes mistress of Johnson Hall, in a strange village full of gluttonous English men and "skinny" slave women, where no women stand "in the door / offering welcome with a hand wave," the marriage ceremony itself reflects a Haudenosaunee reading of this union, where Johnson becomes kin ("My grandfather is now your brother"), and a participant in the world of Mohawk women, with obligations of his own.[19] Molly takes William into her body, her home, her network of relations, her land. Kenny's portrayal is significant in the context of controversy among historians over the nature of their relationship. Although Molly Brant and William Johnson were considered husband and wife under Haudenosauee law, because there was no church wedding or legal union under English law, many historians have characterized Molly as a mistress or concubine, despite the fact that she ran Johnson Hall, was a renowned hostess, had several children with Johnson, and remained with him until his death just before the outbreak of the Revolutionary War. In Kenny's treatment, the Mohawk marriage is fully recognized, and it is made clear how little a church wedding would have meant to the young Molly (although she may have benefited more upon his death had this taken place), and how much Johnson had to gain within Haudenosaunee country by marrying into a Mohawk family and clan.

War, too, is written in a way that represents a sudden emergence into Molly's space, and in these poems, it is juxtaposed with birth in relational opposition. This portrayal reflects the Haudenosaunee story of the twin brothers, Sapling and Flint, who are born of Sky Woman's daughter, representing a dynamic of creation and destruction that is constantly present in Haudenosaunee space. It also adheres to the dynamic between the women's space of the clearing and the men's space of the woods that is an important facet of Haudenosauee social organization.[20] In Kenny's poems, the space of Haudenosaunee women, the fields of fertile corn, the place of birth, is juxtaposed with the space of men and the bloodied fields of battle, which explode during the American Revolution. Molly is a participant in both. From her perspective, the land under siege is exemplified by an empty pot that can barely feed: "the children at the pot / of boiling moss, their supper" and a mother who continues to "stir."[21]

This relational opposition between creation and war is most beautifully developed in the poem "Molly: Passions," which connects the passion for living, for loving, for happiness, for survival, to the defense of land. The poem opens in Molly's exuberant voice, with palpable sensory details:

> Yes, oh yes, passions for blackberry
> blossoms, the clank of deer bones winning games,
> river water sluicing against canoes,
> snow covering old plum trees,
> smells of horse sweat after a fast gallop,
> sounds of mice scratching, the touch of cat fur
> against thighs, good black coffee with sugar.
> I have a passion for hot bread and salty butter
> sweating in brine . . .[22]

In effect, we are immersed in Molly's world of "sensation[s]," the everyday passions that consume her. She is present, vital, alive. In contrast to a narrative flow of dry historical facts about a long dead person on a page, Molly is, as Kenny writes in his preface to the poems, "flesh and bones, blood and guts, truth and physical beauty, wry intellect."[23] We can taste the ripe blackberries (anticipated by flowers), the salty butter, the sharp, sweet coffee. We can sense the rhythmic "sluicing" of water against the canoe, the movement of the horse's rib cage beneath us, the gamblers beside us. We can smell the sweat, the brine. We can hear her voice, clear, assertive, animated. Suddenly, Molly seems more alive than we do, readers of the page. And, as she contradicts the rumors spread about her "fierce passions," whether her desire for her husband, or a demand for an enemy's head, she makes clear that the words of her contemporaries and the subsequent historians cannot be trusted: "They'll say anything to destroy my happiness."

Her "happiness" is directly related to the fecundity of the world that surrounds her; even her marriage to William, the heated desire of it, is connected directly to the reproductive capacity of this world, against which the forces of destruction are juxtaposed:

> I loathe war and blood; I think constantly
> of spring, wind rustling in green corn,
> violets ripening at the wood's edge,
> young possums sucking life into their jaws.

It is in this last line that these oppositions are brought into direct relation: Life so often comes from death, is preserved through violence. Thus, for Molly, it is this very passion for life, wedded to a mother / daughter's fiercely protective impulse, that necessitates war. This irony is present in Molly's mature voice: "I hate war, but love this earth and my kin more / than I hate battles and bravery. This / is my passion . . . to survive with all around me."[24] Thus, it is a desire to sustain all of the life "around" her, the animated world into which she was born, with "all" of her "kin," including those relations now living and those yet to be born, which draws her to participate in war, to "lead an army" who would defend Mohawk lands from the Americans:

> Who would not
> ". . . defend her mother's womb."
> All around me is my mother's womb.
> I lay claim to it.
> This is my passion: life. And the right
> to all it holds: blackberry blossoms,
> marsh iris, the growl of bear at night,
> light rising and falling upon our lodges,
> the rivers that bathe us and slack our thirst,
> and that old plum tree flowering winter with snow.

Here, Molly's position falls in line with other Native women leaders whose presence has been repressed from history. Her words seem to echo those of Nanyehi or Nancy Ward, the Beloved Woman of the Cherokee Nation, who, speaking on behalf of the women's council, implored her relations "not to part with any more of our lands." She urged her "children" to continue to "hold our country in common." To split the nation through removals, to sell lands that belong to the whole, "would be like destroying your mothers."[25] As with the related Cherokees, Haudenosaunee lands rested in the hands of the clan mothers. In Kenny's poem, the rights to the lands which Molly "lay[s] claim to" are based on a deeply rooted genealogy, going all the way back through generations of clan mothers, to Sky Woman, who helped give birth to the world. The political claims of Nancy Ward and Molly Brant are based in kinship, reflecting the mothers' obligation to sustain life in this particular place. These women bear the responsibility of ensuring that the many facets of "life" in this river valley will continue to flourish, on which the survival of future generations depends. This is an obligation held by the "givers of life," and is reflected in the women's own kinship with the womb of their mother, not an abstract "earth" but "this" particular world of their emergence, the Mohawk River, "Te-Non-An-At-Che," and all the life it contains. Furthermore, like Nancy Ward, Molly Brant claims "the right to all it holds" by her genealogy, her descent from the women before her, the "progenitors of nations."[26]

CONFLICT: MOLLY AND THE CLAN MOTHERS

However, strikingly, as Shawnee literary scholar Stephanie Sellers points out, Molly's fellow "progenitors" are noticeably absent from Kenny's poetic portrait. With the possible exception of the Seneca "queen" Aliquippa, Sellers notes, "What appears to be missing from the text are the collective voices of the Mohawk clan mothers." As she demonstrates in her thesis on Kenny's collection, the clan mothers played (and continue to play) a critical role in the Haudenosaunee political system, and are among the many Native women who have often been repressed from the narratives of American history. As Sellers explores the historical role of women in the Confederacy and their subsequent erasure, speculating on several places where their voices might be implied, she ponders, "Still I must wonder why [Kenny] does not make an explicit statement from the women's council of Tekonwatonti's era in order to demonstrate the significant role that council played in both the politics of the time and in the Iroquois Confederacy in particular."[27]

One possible answer to Seller's question lies in the conflict between Molly Brant and the clan mothers prior to and during the Revolutionary War. If they were to make a collective statement in poetic voice, it might very well be in disagreement with Brant. As the Revolutionary War began brewing in the colonies, British loyalists and colonial rebels competed for Haudenosaunee support. The Confederacy's position, like that of many Native nations in the east, was to maintain a position of neutrality, urging their relations not to "intermeddle in this dispute between two brothers."[28] This decision rested with the clan mothers, who had the sole authority to determine whether the collective nations of the Confederacy should pursue war. There were numerous councils held from 1774 to 1776, and the clan mothers repeatedly confirmed their stance, making it clear that any of the young men who struck off and joined either the British or the American forces would be doing so on their own, against the wishes of their leadership. Molly Brant's brother, Joseph, was one of these young men. He had traveled to London with the sons-in-law of William Johnson, and became convinced that continuing the Mohawk alliance with the British Crown was the best strategy for the defense of Mohawk lands. In recruiting warriors at Oquaga, Brant reportedly said that they should "defend their Lands & Liberty against the Rebels, who in a great measure began this Rebellion to be sole Masters of this Continent."[29]

Although he was acting against the decision of the clan mothers, Brant's actions were in line with his sister's position. From the beginning, Molly rallied to the British side, in part because of her kinship ties to Johnson's family, in part because, she, like Joseph, believed that this was the best strategy for the protection of Mohawk lands. At a critical council at German Flatts, on the Mohawk River, just before the influential Albany Treaty, one of the American representatives observed, "The Indians pay her great respect and I am afraid her influence will give us some trouble." Molly remained at her home village of Canajoharie protecting her own matrilineal inheritance (as well as the wealth she had inherited from her husband) from colonial armies long after many other families had left. She abandoned her substantial house, with her seven children, only after the Confederacy divided and the clan mothers abandoned the position of neutrality. Oneida warriors struck her home at Canajoharie after she sent messengers to alarm the Mohawk and British warriors of the approach of American troops, resulting in an ambush at Oriskany. Even after her home was hit, Molly remained confident of her eventual return, writing to (Johnson's son-in-law) Daniel Claus, "I hope the Time is very near, when we shall all return to our habitations on the Mohawk River." Joining other refugees at Niagara, Molly played an instrumental leadership role in maintaining Haudenosaunee support for the British cause. During the many large councils that were held there during the war, she acted as "confidant in every Matter of Importance & was consulted thereupon." Reflecting on her influence among the male leadership of the Confederacy, Claus related that, "one word from her is more taken Notice of by the five Nations than a thousand from any white Man without exception."[30]

Yet, in these poems, Joseph bears the brunt of the blame for complicity with the division of the Confederacy and the destruction of his kin and homeland. The poem "Thayendanegea / Joseph Brant" is simply a single quote: "I love the English. / I give them everything."[31] In "A Warrior on Joseph Brant," the speaker indicts the young leader who would "kill thy people in hallucination; / kill the earth in foolishness . . . spit on the moon whose nipples / feed the young."[32] It is Joseph's allegiance to "Your British" which results in the rampant devastation: "Fields rust, rivers decay; sky / explodes, women birth barren. The Longhouse sputters / in leaping flames." In contrast, Molly appears to be more righteous, more deserving of our sympathy than her brother, caught in a whirlwind of war and expressing an ambivalent pride for these "young men" who she "lead[s]" into "battle, victory— / perhaps death." Devastated by the violence and loss around her, she acknowledges her brother and the other warriors "fight for England now / but truly for the survival of the Longhouse."[33]

However, Molly's own opposition to the decision of the clan mothers is absent. In giving truth to the substantial authority that Molly swayed during these tumultuous times, Kenny elides the role of the women who collectively strove for the maintenance of the Confederacy against the two powers that pulled on its doors, perhaps erasing the conflicts between women leaders in order to honor one. Still, the greatest point that Kenny makes, particularly in his complex portrayal of Molly during the war, is that all of these female leaders were motivated by protection and defense of land and kin above all else. Whether their strategy was swift and steadfast alliance with the British or steady neutrality, it was their responsibility and claim to all "life" in their "mother's womb" that was at the root of their decisions, and their passionate defense of those positions, even against each other.

In Kenny's Haudenosaunee interpretation, even William Johnson is motivated by the desire to protect his Mohawk River lands. In "Molly," the heroine's voice speaks in defense of her late husband: "Willie, they say / you would have fought for / the British . . . I say, and I know . . . you would have / fought / for freedom . . . if only your own; / aimed a rifle to protect your / fields." In this poem, Johnson's desire to protect his property, including his "mansion," his "silver and slaves," is connected to the defense of Mohawk lands. Like the Mohawks, Johnson too, is allied with the "British" who "were never friends," but "coveted your fields and grain," while "the colonists needed your fortitude." This position not only complicates Molly's own alliance with the British, but Johnson's and her nation's as a whole, reflecting the thorny relationship between the Mohawks and the English settlers over an extended period of time. Although allies in trade and war, the British posed a constant threat to Mohawk territorial sovereignty and subsistence. Molly even speculates that had Johnson lived to see the war, and chosen to fight "against the crown / our people, my people, would be / as resilient now / as they were the day you / entered this valley / with dreams and cunning, / smiling, grinning bravely."[34] Through Molly's eyes, Johnson is viewed as an inhabitant of the valley, interwoven in the fabric of kinship of which she also is a part. Even as the poet paints a portrait of "Willie" that suggests his desire for women is as insatiable as his desire for land, from Molly's position of loyalty, even Johnson's desire to maintain his property is tied in defense to claims of her own.

This loyalty to land and kin ultimately is what connects Molly to the clan mothers that were her contemporaries, even when they found themselves on opposite sides of a war. As the Seneca leader Aliquippa's voices rises from "Steel Town, Pennsylvania," it is "the earth, the earth / and all it contains" that motivates and unites their actions:

> For this Molly rode her black horse;
> for this alone I crept on hands and knees
> through forests of bramble and prickles,
> bloodied my face and hands. We ridiculed our men
> to follow our lead, as all women must. Were we
> not the heads of our clans, obliged to prod
> the men to hunt or war to feed and protect
> the village our hands constructed, our wombs
> populated, our mind furbished?

Again, as with the many Molly poems, it is "this earth," this Mohawk land, the villages held and built by women, for which these wars are fought. In this poem, Aliquippa joins Molly in reclaiming the role of women leaders, which have been all but eradicated from the historical record. She insists of their quest for continuance: "This was history. Not the dates / of battles, nor names of generals, nor flags unfurled over towns and valleys; nor river soiled / with the blood of French Jesuits or Delawares. / I did not fight beside the young George / Washington because of his comely face."

In an article on *Tekonwatonti / Molly Brant* published in *MELUS*, Patrick Barron asks why Kenny does not locate Molly's life in the history of the "inter-tribal wars" of the seventeenth and eighteenth centuries, a favored period for academic historians, wondering whether Kenny represses this standard history "because it rests uneasily with his image of the Iroquois nation."[35] However, Kenny's approach follows that of Haudenosaunee oratorical and written tradition, locating Molly's life within a longstanding framework of Haudenosaunee historical narration, beginning with the Sky Woman story, and centered on the formation of the Great Law and the continuity of the Confederacy through periods of challenge and change.[36] Thus, the poem "Aliquippa," transfers our attention from the "dates / ," "names," "flags," and "blood of Jesuits and Delawares" to "the Longhouse" to "hear the words / once more of the great Peacemaker." To the story of the "great turtle," and the "prayers of the woman / who fell from the sky heavy with child"; to the regeneration of the land and the "'*Haudenosauee*,' people of the longhouse" which she can foresee: "I know, I am Aliquippa / and I have said this will happen." In this poem, which represents the last voice to speak from the ashes of the Revolution, the story ends not with the termination of Mohawk lands, the termination of the Confederacy and an era of Haudenosaunee sovereignty, but with a clear and insistent vision of regeneration, which is carefully constructed by Kenny to be a future already certain, a Mohawk place that is already in transformation, returning to its eternal state:

> Air will clear, eagle take the highest branch
> of the white pine, hawk alight
> on the elm as the river runs swiftly below
> sparkling with speckled trout.

Of course, this is a world that Kenny has already seen, and in this moment, the poet is united with his subject, in the place of their birth, death, and regeneration. Although some may consider this an idealistic portrayal, Kenny has seen much come to pass in his lifetime, including the reclamations of Mohawk lands at Ganienkeh and Kanatsiohareke, as well as the defense of sovereignty at Oka and Kahnawake, inspired and led by Haudenosaunee clan mothers.

This foregrounding of Molly's and Aliquippa's voices brings Haudenosaunee women's roles as rememberers to the center. As Kenny writes in "Women-Memory," "While the men / were the tongues / of the Confederacy, / the women / were the ears." The speaker in "Doug George, Historian" observes "The pages of our oral chronicles / simmer with voices / and stories of our women. / (Why doesn't the world hear them?)"[37] The voice of "Aliquippa" resounds, bridging past and present: "We will have forgotten nothing."[38] When Haudenosaunee speakers were sent to councils to represent the words of the whole, they were always accompanied by a group of women, whose role it was to remember and record the words exchanged, to bring back these words to the councils of the Confederacy, for deliberation and remembrance. As a young woman, Molly herself had participated in such a council, accompanying her mother's husband and her clan chief Hendrick on a diplomatic trip to Philadelphia in 1755, to discuss a longstanding dispute over fraudulent land sales.[39] The restoration of this role, through poetic imagination, brings her into "her rightful place" as a rememberer, retrieving that power from those historians who simplified and caricatured her on the page, even making her into an object of their own desires. As Kenny writes in "What the Chroniclers Did Not Record," like many such 'subjects,' "She had nothing to fear but history / the paws of scholars on her grave." In this endeavor, Kenny is part of an important movement in Haudenosaunee history-making: an effort by Haudenosaunee leaders, writers, and scholars to reclaim and renew women's roles in Haudenosaunee history, and to practice "intellectual sovereignty" in the process of remembering.[40] In these poems, "Molly" reclaims her desire as her own, and transforms it to the regeneration of nations. And, as Stephanie Sellers observes, her descendants are myriad: "Native women living today are as much a part of the story of Tekonwatonti as she is of their story." Thus Kenny's penultimate section "Women / Memory," contains the voices of "generations," including "E. Pauline Johnson (1861–1919)," the Mohawk poet, whose "mind is fettered with Molly" and "Jennie (Parker Herrick) Sanford, Age 82," from "Carleton Island," the place where Molly lived and died long after the close of the Revolutionary War, who remarks, "My nephew claims I am the family historian. / I don't know about that, but my head buzzes, voices / echo and re-echo and reverberate." And, finally, the poet himself, "Sitting in the Waters of the Grasse River," near the Akwesasne reserve, where the waters of the old St. Lawrence River face industrial pollution beyond measure, impacting not only the health and survival water animals and fish, but the human inhabitants of the reserve as well.[41] Here,

> Louie and I sit in the warm waters of the rapids
> soaping our hair and talking of Molly.
> One thought creates another,
> One word builds a bridge between two minds,
> Two ages, centuries spanning Molly and us.[42]

Although "the Mohawk, like the Grasse where we now sit," is "so clogged" that "no bass can breathe, no turtle spawn / in the wastes and poisons dumped by a thoughtless society," its regenerative, life-insistent flow continues, and Molly's descendants are embedded participants in the "drop / drop / drop" of its course:

> . . . Upstream we see the canoe
> flowing toward us. The finch still feeds in the air
> and blackcaps continue to ripen.
> Louie and I rinse out the soap, refreshed now
> leave dripping war on the shore,
> thankful for the cool rapids.[43]

PAINTING "WORD-PICTURES" IN PLACE

In talking about his role as a composer of "poetic history," Kenny relayed in an interview with Chad Sweeney that he could see parallels between *Tekonwatonti / Molly Brant* and his current project, *Conversations with Frida Kahlo: Collage of Memory*. He reflected:

> in researching and writing about Frida I was really looking for Molly Brant again. I sat in the main plaza in Coyoacán, and down the road was Frida's house, and over there was Malinche's house, and up there was Trotsky's house, and Diego had a house there, too. Ah, the waves that came across that plaza! It was shaking the flowers and trees there! Fantastic! I was just seething with inspiration. I couldn't wait to start writing.[44]

There is a way that Kenny is moved, pulled by the power of place and the "echoes" they retain to bring these stories to the page, to recreate the images that emerge in his mind from his own interaction with the places to which these women belong. With Sweeney, he discussed the "many kinds of truth" and his own methodology in drawing poetic truth from particular places. Sweeney asked, "What can you do that historians haven't been able to do?" Kenny replied, "Go into the garden and sit. Historians don't *paint* pictures. They *tell* pictures. I tried to get into her soul, through my soul. Through my lust I tried to get into her lust. Through my pain I tried to get to her pain."[45]

This is poetry that relies on imagination, imagery, and intimacy with its subjects. "There is a need to touch," the poet softly proclaims.[46] Kenny has called himself a "painter of word-pictures," yet, the pictures he creates are not landscapes, which allow us to view figures like Molly from a distance, but "word-paintings" embedded in particular environments, which skillfully draw the reader into them. Not only does the author practice empathy, but he compels the reader to do so, as well. Kenny creates evocative image-portraits in words, based on extensive historical research and intimate understanding of place. We scholars owe a great debt, and have much to learn, from creative writers like him.

Kenny's methodology is important for those of us who wish to continue the work of Indigenous history, creative writing, and even literary criticism. This process requires imagination, and an effort to put ourselves in place, which is quite different from the scholar's quest for objectivity and distance. Many Native poets have followed this course in parallel with Kenny, from Simon Ortiz's *from Sand Creek* and Joy Harjo's classic "New Orleans," to Cheryl Savageau's recently published *Mother / land*.[47] However, we also are seeing a surge in scholarly work that takes this approach, including Daniel Justice's empathetic, complex portrait of a Cherokee literary tradition in *Our Fire Survives the Storm* and Craig Womack's *Art as Performance, Story as Criticism* in which he explicitly seeks to write about literature using the fiction writer's imaginative and empathetic lens.[48] These poets and creative scholars seek "many kinds of truth," which are drawn out through empathy and creativity rather than objectivity, in dialogue with both their subjects and their readers. Importantly, however, these works not only bridge the "distance" between past and present through acts of imagination, but through putting themselves, literally, in the places of the people about whom they are writing. In their evocative portrayals of their own perceptions in place, we, as readers, are brought into these places and made to experience them with new vision.

In Kenny's work, this craft of creating "word-pictures" in place is rooted both in modernist imagism and Indigenous pictographic writing. Kenny, like his heroine Aliquippa, seeks neither "honor nor loot" but "only to write / on the rock, paint color for the grandchildren."[49] He is a master of using words to create images in his reader's mind that transform our perception of place. Consider the following short poem:

Albany:
a nest of crawling
copperheads.

This portrait brings an immediate, arresting image to mind. In it, we can see the influence of American modernist literature (think William Carlos Williams's "Red Wheelbarrow"), and that of classical Indigenous graphic arts.[50] Albany is characterized in many histories as a center of trade and treaties, colonial development, burgeoning democracy; a place of emergence for the United States. But Kenny uses his word painting to displace this image, and fill our minds with another, which instantly takes shape in our mind's eye. The poem works like a glyphic representation of place: "Albany" is the image of a twisted mass of dangerous snakes, which can come at you unsuspectingly, which you might naïvely come across; which hide in the crevices of rock outcroppings, and appear suddenly before you. As a poet, Kenny makes us stop and think: What does it mean for "Albany" to be "a nest"of "crawling" snakes? What would it feel like to come across, or be embroiled in, this nest? Through such images, we see his craft: He seduces us into the historical landscape of his Mohawk ancestors with lustrous detail. As Kenny paints these portraits of places, as he calls the names of water plants, rivers, streams, and villages, they are implanted in our minds, and the landscape is transformed.

There is a delicate beauty even in his intimate description of an unnamed Native woman's death in "New Amsterdam, 1652":

> At Cedar Street and Trinity Place
> Hendrick Van Dyck raised his old musket
> into position; sight fixed
> he shot her dead. A single peach clutched
> in her hand, her braided hair
> streamed in her own blood,
> her face a map of twisting paths. . .
> Today we are denied her name;
> the Dutch chose not to record it.
> But her dissidence, her act
> is remembered and honored
> and her hungry children survived
> to tell her story—a single Indian hand
> raised into green leaves to fetch life.[51]

This woman, whose only appearance in the historical record is her death for "stealing" a peach, is only one of many Native women who Kenny revives in memory and imagination, through provocative portraits in place. He marks the site, in the contemporary metropolis of Manhattan, reminding us of its location in colonial history. Through his style of "word-painting," Kenny firmly lodges the image of this nameless woman in our minds, along with the significance of her death, and her survival, through her "children" and the portrait that her living descendant creates. Now, when we walk through these streets, we will be participants in the process of remembering.

Yet, the most striking portraits in the collection are of his main subject. Through Kenny's songs, "Molly" appears to attempt to bridge the gap between her time and ours, between her children and the descendants of the Colonists who are claiming her homeland. Like the artist-historian, she seeks to record her impressions "onto birchbark or rock," so that "you would remember always / where your freedoms and liberties / first captured your attention." Molly wishes to literally "scratch" her impressions on a surface more permanent than paper, the history of "how my many grandfathers struggled / to construct the Longhouse / a central fire with two doors / which you entered and from which / you took out a lit kindling." As she tells it, her ancestors are the true "fathers of Thirteen Fires," the United States, which during her time, were attempting to overtake Mohawk lands. As we discover in an earlier piece, "Washington" was "standing on turtle." The poem "Molly" is a brilliant northeastern Native rendering of the relationship between Molly's kin and the Americans who attempted to "replace" them, demonstrating the place of Americans in the network of relations: children to the "fathers" who came before them, who exist before them in "this earth on turtle's back."[52]

As with the first poem of the collection, multiple times are layered in this one place, multiple generations connected through their relationship to a specific environment. Molly speaks to "you," the generations that are alive now, directly. And she speaks quite exclusively, not to the generations of Mohawks who remain here and throughout the continent, but to the descendants of "Albany" who have forgotten their place in a Haudenosaunee historical landscape, have forgotten their own origin story in this land they now claim. Yet, she does not wish for their obliteration, but continues to honor the ideal of the Covenant Chain, the alliance her ancestors made so long ago: "May your fire burn / and allow our fire / to blaze as well." The fire here is no mere symbol, but a metonym for the political system of the Haudenosaunee Confederacy, which exists in the same space with the government of the United States. Her words recall the image of the Two-Row Wampum, which recorded the mutual pledge of the English colonists and the Haudenosaunee to pursue parallel paths, each in its own canoe, without interfering with the other's course. Like many Native orators before and after her, she does not cry out for pity, or for guilt, only for the honoring of an old agreement. And as many of the writers and orators in the northeast would remind their contemporaries, Molly concludes by assuring her audience that their forgetting may come around to haunt them, with a line set aside from the rest of the verse:

> A people who do not remember:
> *rain which falls upon a rock.*[53]

Here, again, we have the movement of water, just as in the opening poem. Yet, this flow suggests transciency, rather than continuance. Unlike her "figures" etched permanently on rock and the wampum belts that permanently record the history and laws of the Confederacy, the "Americans" and their stories may fade away, a brief period in a long Indigenous history. She warns that the failure to remember may lead to the failure to persist. Memory is connected to survival. Furthermore, with this line, Kenny completes an important reversal. Native people often are characterized as a people without history, whose oral traditions only can preserve the memory of a few generations. Countless historians bemoan the fact that Native people left no records of their experience, that there are few Native accounts to be accessed in reconstructing history. Kenny's reminds his audience of the long tradition of "remembers" among nations like the Mohawk, aided by mnemonic tools like wampum belts, which created images associated with words in the minds of its holders, and listeners who continue to gather annually to participate in communal remembrance. Kenny, a participant himself in these gatherings, plays his own part. Rather than using images to recall words, Kenny uses words to create images, which will work in our own minds, so that we may recall and remember the history that is still very much alive in this place.

NOTES

1. Lisa Brooks, *The Common Pot: The Recovery of Native Space in the Northeast* (Minneapolis: University of Minnesota Press, 2008), 120–121, The question "where are your women?" was famously asked by the Cherokee leader Ada-gal'kala, or Attakullakulla, at a council with the English in the eighteenth century. See Marilou Awiakta, *Selu: Seeking the Corn-Mother's Wisdom* (Golden, CO: Fulcrum, 1993), 92; Daniel Justice, *Our Fire Survives the Storm: A Cherokee Literary History* (Minneapolis: University of Minnesota Press, 2006), 31–32, 35. Sally Roesch Wagner, *Sisters in Spirit: Haudenosaunee (Iroquois) Influences on Early American Feminists* (Summertown TN: Book Publishing Company, 2001).

2. Maurice Kenny, *Tekonwatonti/Molly Brant: Poems of War* (Buffalo, NY: White Pine Press, 1992), 12. As Kenny notes in his preface, "In research, one book was found devoted to Molly, a novel published in 1951 based, perhaps, on hearsay or legend with few facts." This novel was Margaret Widdemer's *Lady of the Mohawks*, which Kenny quotes in a poem near the opening of the collection. Kenny conducted extensive historical research in primary and secondary sources, which occasionally appear in direct quotes in his poetry. Throughout the collection, his commitment to accuracy and integrity in his representation of Molly as a real historical personage is evident. Since Kenny's publication, several scholarly articles and at least one book devoted to Molly Brant have appeared, including: Lois M. Huey and Bonnie Pulis, *Molly Brant: A Legacy of Her Own* (Youngstown, NY: Old Fort Niagara Association); Lois M. Feister and Bonnie Pulis, "Molly Brant: Her Domestic and Political Roles in Eighteenth-Century New York," in Robert Steven Grumet, ed., *Northeastern Indian Lives, 1632–1816* (Amherst: University of Massachusetts Press, 1996), 295–320; Gretchen Green, "Molly Brant, Catharine Brant, and Their Daughters: A Study in Colonial Acculturation," *Ontario History* LXXXI, no. 3 (September 1989), 235–250 (This essay was published before Kenny's publication, but many years after he embarked on historical research.)

3. Chad Sweeney, "An Interview with Maurice Kenny," *World Literature Today* 79 (May 2005), 66.

4. Maurice Kenny, "Waiting at the Edge: Words toward a Life," *I Tell You Now: Autobiographical Essays By Native American Writers*, ed. Brian Swann and Arnold Krupat (Lincoln: University of Nebraska Press, 1987), 40.

5. Kenny, *Tekonwatonti/Molly Brant*, 19.

6. Kenny, *Tekonwatonti/Molly Brant*, 20–22.

7. Kenny was born "in the foothills of the Adirondacks on the shores of the Black River." The St. Lawrence River was a major Indigenous trade route and is the location of the Mohawk reservation of Akwesasne, one of many places Kenny calls

"home." The Genesee, like the Black, flows into Lake Ontario, but from Seneca country, his mother's line. The Blue is another tributary of the Mohawk, flowing from the north. Swann 45–46; Joseph Bruchac, "Our Own Pasts: An Interview with Maurice Kenny," *Survival This Way: Interviews with American Indian Poets* (Tucson: University of Arizona Press, 1987), 151.

8. Kenny, *Tekonwatonti/Molly Brant*, 20–22.

9. Ibid., 21.

10. This line recalls the Abenaki story of the Chenoo, or "Ice-Heart," often told by Joseph Bruchac, with which Kenny may be quite familiar. See Joseph Bruchac, The Ice-Hearts (Austin, TX: Cold Mountain Press, 1979).

11. Ibid., 22.

12. See, for instance, Mark Warhus, *Another America: Native American Maps and the History of Our Land* (New York: St. Martin's Griffin, 1997), 77–82.

13. Kenny, *Tekonwatonti/Molly Brant*, 68.

14. I draw this phrase from historian Jean O'Brien's work. See Jean M. O'Brien, "'Vanishing' Indians in Nineteenth-Century New England: Local Historians' Erasure of Still-Present Indian Peoples," in Sergei A. Kan and Pauline Turner Strong, *New Perspectives on Native North America: Cultures, Histories, and Representations* (Lincoln: University of Nebraska Press, 2006). Thanks very much to Jeani for sharing her work, as well, at a presentation she gave at Harvard University in February 2006, entitled "New England Local Histories as Replacement Narratives." For a full treatment of this phenomenon, see Jean O'Brien, *Firsting and Lasting* (Minneapolis: University of Minnesota Press, 2010).

15. Kenny, *Tekonwatonti/Molly Brant*, 57.

16. Ibid., 62. Seneca Arthur Parker's recorded version of the Great Law states that the "lineal descent . . . shall run in the female line. Women shall be considered the progenitors of the Nation. They shall own the land and the soil. Men and women shall follow the status of their mother." Arthur Caswell Parker, "The Constitution of the Five Nations," Parker on the Iroquois, ed. William Fenton (Syracuse, NY: Syracuse University Press, 1968)., 42.

17. Ibid, 63.

18. Ibid., 65.

19. Ibid., 66, 65.

20. See Akwesasne Notes, ed., *Basic Call to Consciousness* (Summertown, TN: Book Publishing Co., 1991). Kevin A. Connelly, "The Textual Function of Onondaga Aspect, Mood, and Tense: A Journey into Onondaga Conceptual Space," PhD Dissertation, Cornell University, 1999. Demus Elm, Harvey Antone, Floyd Glenn Lounsbury and Bryan Gick, *The Oneida Creation Story* (Lincoln: University of Nebraska Press, 2000). William N. Fenton, *The Great Law and the Longhouse: A Political History of the Iroquois Confederacy* (Norman: University of Oklahoma Press, 1998). Francis Jennings, *The Ambiguous Iroquois Empire: The Covenant Chain Confederation of Indian Tribes with English Colonies from Its Beginnings to the Lancaster Treaty of 1744* (New York: Norton, 1984). Oren Lyons, ed., *Exiled in the Land of the Free: Democracy, Indian Nations, and the U.S. Constitution* (Santa Fe, NM: Clear Light Publishers, 1992). Barbara Mann, *Iroquois Women: The Gantowisas* (New York: Peter Lang, 2004). John Mohawk, "A View from Turtle Island: Chapters in Iroquois Mythology, History, and Culture," Phd Dissertation, SUNY Buffalo, 1993.

John Mohawk, *Iroquois Creation Story: John Arthur Gibson and J.N.B. Hewitt's Myth of the Earth Grasper* (Buffalo, NY: Mohawk Publications, 2005). Parker, "Constitution." Arthur Caswell Parker, *Seneca Myths and Folk Tales* (Lincoln: University of Nebraska Press, 1989), 59–73. Daniel K. Richter, *The Ordeal of the Longhouse: The Peoples of the Iroquois League in the Era of European Colonization* (Chapel Hill: University of North Carolina Press, 1992). Joanne Shenandoah and Douglas M. George, *Sky Woman: Legends of the Iroquois (Santa Fe: Clear Light Publishers, 1998)*. Robert W. Venables, "Some Observations on the Treaty of Canadaigua," *Treaty of Canadaigua 1794*, ed. G. Peter Jemison and Anna M. Schein (Santa Fe, NM: Clear Light Publishing, 2000). Paul Wallace, *White Roots of Peace* (Santa Fe, NM: Clear Light Publishers, 1994).

21. Kenny, *Tekonwatonti/Molly Brant*, 140.

22. Ibid., 144.

23. Ibid., 12.

24. Ibid., 145.

25. Karen L. Kilcup, ed., *Native American Women Writers, c. 1800–1924: An Anthology* (Malden, MA: Blackwell, 2000), 26–30. On Nanyehi, see Awiakta, Selu, 92–106; Justice, Our Fire, 31–42.

26. See note 16 above. See also Mann, *Iroquois Women*; Sally Roesch Wagner, *Sisters in Spirit: Haudenosaunee (Iroquois) Influences on Early American Feminists* (TN: Book Publishing Company, 2001).

27. Stephanie Ann Sellers, "Redefining Native American Autobiography: The Case of Tekonwatonti," PhD Dissertation, Union Institute, 2004, 86–87.

28. "Oneidas' Declaration of Neutrality . . . to the Four New England Colonies," *American Archives*, 1st ser., 4:116–117.

29. Colin G. Calloway, *The American Revolution in Indian Country: Crisis and Diversity in Native Americans Communities* (Cambridge, England; New York: Cambridge University Press, 1995). 122–123. See also Barbara Graymont, *The Iroquois in the American Revolution* (Syracuse, NY: Syracuse University Press, 1972); Mann, *Iroquois Women*.

30. Calloway, American., 129, 134–6, and Chapter Five generally; Graymont, *Iroquois*, 13, 47, 157–161; Feister and Pulis, "Molly Brant," 306–313; Green, "Molly Brant," 239–241; Huey and Pulis, *Molly*, 43–44, 49, 53, 107; Barbara Graymont, "Konwatsi?tsianiénni" in *Dictionary of Candian Biography*, © 2000 University of Toronto/Université Laval. http://www.biographi.ca/EN/ShowBio.asp?BioId=36113&query=molly%20AND%20brant (August 7, 2006)

31. Kenny, *Tekonwatonti/Molly Brant*, 138.

32. Ibid., 139.

33. Ibid., 146–147.

34. Ibid., 151.

35. Patrick Barron, "Maurice Kenny's *Tekonwatonti/Molly Brant*: Poetic Memory and History," *MELUS* 25:3/4 (Fall/Winter 2000), 42.

36. See, for example, John Norton, Carl Frederick Klinck and James John Talman, *The Journal of Major John Norton, 1816* (Toronto: Champlain Society, 1970). David Cusick, *Sketches of Ancient History of the Six Nations: Comprising a Tale of the Foundation of the Great Island (Now North America), the Two Infants Born, and the Creation of the Universe* (Lockport, NY: Niagara Country Historical Society, 1961). Parker, "Constitution." Parker, *Seneca Myths*, 59–73. Akwesasne Notes, *Basic Call.*

See also William N. Fenton, "Structure, Continuity, and Change in the Process of Iroquois Treaty Making," in *The History and Culture of Iroquois Diplomacy*, ed. Francis Jennings and William N. Fenton (Syracuse, NY: Syracuse University Press, 1985), 13.

37. Kenny, *Tekonwatonti/Molly Brant*, 50.

38. Ibid., 179.

39. Barbara Graymont, "Konwatsi?tsianiénni. See also Feister and Pulis, "Molly Brant," Green, "Molly Brant," Mann, Iroquois Women.

40. Kenny, *Tekonwatonti/Molly Brant*, 168. I draw the phrase "her rightful place" from the work of Tuscarora historian Alyssa Mt. Pleasant. In addition to her dissertation, Mt. Pleasant is engaged in historical recovery of the role of Jigonsaseh, a co-founder of the Confederacy and a political position held by the leading clan mother in each generation. See "After the Whirlwind: Maintaining a Haudenosaunee Place at Buffalo Creek, 1780–1825," PhD Dissertation, Cornell University, 2007 and an unpublished essay, "Searching for Her Rightful Place: Jigonsaseh's Legacy Amongst the Haudenosaunee." Special thanks to Alyssa for sharing her work with me. See also, for example, Taiaiake Alfred, *Peace, Power, Righteousness: An Indigenous Manifesto* (New York: Oxford University Press, 1999); Jose Barriero, ed., *Indian Roots of American Democracy* (Ithaca, NY: Akwekon Press, Cornell University, 1992); G. Peter Jemison and Anna M. Schein, eds., *Treaty of Canandaigua 1794* (Santa Fe, NM: Clear Light Publishers, 2000); Lyons, ed. *Exiled*; Mann, *Iroquois Women*; Wagner, *Sisters in Spirit*. Robert Warrior developed the concept of "intellectual sovereignty" in *Tribal Secrets: Recovering American Indian Intellectual Traditions* (Minneapolis: University of Minnesota Press, 1995), in which he called on literary critics to "practice the same sort of intellectual sovereignty" that he saw "many Native poets" already accomplishing.

41. Kenny, *Tekonwatonti/Molly Brant*, 194. See Winona LaDuke, "Akwesasne: Mother's Milk and PCBs" in *All Our Relations: Native Struggles for Land and Life* (Boston: South End Press, 1999); Bruce Johansen, *Life and Death in Mohawk Country* (Golden, CO: Fulcrum, 2006).

42. Kenny, *Tekonwatonti/Molly Brant*, 194.

43. Ibid., 195.

44. Chad Sweeney, "An Interview with Maurice Kenny," *World Literature Today* 79 (May 2005), 68.

45. Ibid., 66.

46. Kenny, *Tekonwatonti/Molly Brant*, 193.

47. See Simon Ortiz, *from Sand Creek* (Tucson: University of Arizona Press, 1981); Joy Harjo, "New Orleans," in Joseph Bruchac, ed. *Songs from this Earth on Turtle's Back* (Greenfield Center, NY: Greenfield Review Press, 1983); Cheryl Savageau, *Mother/land* (Cambridge, England: Salt Publishing, 2006).

48. Justice, Our Fire. See note 1, above. Craig Womack, *Art as Performance, Story as Criticism* (Norman: University of Oklahoma Press, 2009).

49. Kenny, *Tekonwatonti/Molly Brant*, 176.

50. Bruchac, *Survival*, 150.

51. Kenny, *Tekonwatonti/Molly Brant*, 30.

52. Ibid., 129, 130, 152–3. See note 14, for the notion of "replacement." See also note 36, for "this Earth on Turtle's Back."

53. Kenny, Tekonwatonti/Molly Brant, 130.

TEN

TWO-SPIRIT IMAGES IN THE WORK OF MAURICE KENNY

Lisa Tatonetti

A poet, fiction writer, essayist, editor, and publisher, Mohawk author Maurice Kenny has done it all in his prolific career. He published his first full-length collection, *Dead Letters Sent*, in 1958, the same year as the chapbook *With Love to Lesbia* and released his latest book, *Connotations*, in 2008 as a companion to the award-winning and recently re-issued *Mama Poems* (1984).[1] The fifty years between *Dead Letters Sent* and *Connotations* are filled with multiple collections of powerful poetry, prose, and essays, alongside anthologies and edited editions of literature both compiled by and including Kenny. There are also bits and pieces of memoir and interview to be found in the body of Kenny's work. For example, in his 1995 collection, *On Second Thought,* Maurice Kenny delights the reader with a sixty-some page introduction that meanders through his experiences as a poet and essayist. Taking us frankly from his difficult early years as a struggling student, to his days as the manager of the 57th Street Marboro bookstore in New York City and into his adult life as a successful poet, Kenny shares his life, a few loves, and, most importantly, the development of his literary voice and career. In this and other autobiographical pieces, Kenny makes clear that his focus is on both the craft of writing and on his ties to the Mohawk nation and, particularly to the land and people of Akwesasne, the St. Regis Mohawk reservation that sits on a confluence of rivers in the St. Lawrence River Valley. The stories and images of this landscape permeate Kenny's prose and such themes are key to Kenny's work. However, in this chapter, I suggest that alongside, and sometimes entwined, with these images of land and nation are stirring metaphors of Two-Spirit desire. Rarely discussed, these metaphors represent an important way in which Kenny has influenced the field of Indigenous literature.

One of the ways in which Kenny's impact has been felt in the field of Native literature has been in his willingness to break boundaries and forge new ground. And such was definitely the case in 1976 when Kenny published a critical essay, "Tinseled Bucks: A Historical Study of Indian Homosexuality," and a poem, "Winkte," in Winston Leyland's landmark journal of queer literature, *Gay Sunshine*. As the first pieces of contemporary queer Native literature to be published, these texts function as the cornerstone of what has since become a significant body of work.[2] Thus, although Two-Spirit sexuality is not an overt theme in the majority of Kenny's work, he stands together with writers like Beth Brant (Bay of Quinte Mohawk), Paula Gunn Allen (Laguna Pueblo), and Chrystos (Menominee) as one of the earliest contemporary Native writers to address Two-Spirit desire at a time in which such conversations were not being brought into the public sphere.[3]

Only a year before Kenny published his pieces in *Gay Sunshine*, the first organization for lesbian, gay, bisexual, transgender, and queer (LGBTQ) Native people in the United States, Gay American Indians (GAI), was cofounded by Randy Burns (Paiute) and Barbara Cameron (Lakota) in 1975.

In the memoir with which he begins his 1995 *On Second Thought*, Kenny talks of meeting Cameron and Burns, together with Sharol Graves (Crow), describing them as "young, beautiful people centered in their cultures, eager to give back to their cultures as they had been gifted with so much," and calling the mid-1970s a time during which a "world opened, and a prism of light and color pervaded this world."[4] Although Kenny does not directly address the GAI, he speaks of this era as one of camaraderie and discovery, saying "In those days there weren't many Native writers who were published. We were friends and helped each other by suggesting publications and readings. We shared what little was out there."[5] Throughout the memoir, Kenny emphasizes cultural continuity, interpersonal connection, and the centrality of indigeneity when he speaks of the community of Native writers he embraced during this period. He clearly cherishes the ties he made with other American Indian writers, both because of the people they were (regardless of cultural background) and because of their ties to their various tribal nations. He says "I was in a circle, a sacred circle of life with like kind, my own kind, native poets. I was no more the loner, the outlaw, nor even delinquent."[6] Unsurprisingly, this focus comes to the fore in several of the pieces in which Kenny addresses Two-Spirit desire.

BREAKING BARRIERS: BRINGING TWO-SPIRIT DESIRE TO LIGHT

Kenny's poem "Winkte" is in many ways a literary parallel to his scholarly work in the essay "Tinseled Bucks." Both of these pieces are revisionist histories that speak to the historical erasure of Indian queerness by reclaiming the place of gender variance in Indigenous history and refuting the prevalent idea that homosexuality and / or gender variance is a "white man's disease." Published in the same winter 1975 / 1976 issue of *Gay Sunshine*, these pieces are both a statement of fact and a call to arms when one considers the climate of the times. In "Tinseled Bucks," Kenny first critiques the elision of much of the historical record about Two-Spirit people and roles, suggesting that "manifestation[s] of male love" were often "ignore[d]" and considered an unacceptable "subject for the official record."[7] The essay goes on to review some of the existing historical documents from the nineteenth and early twentieth centuries that detail the existence of Two-Spirit people among a number of tribes. Kenny notes the varying tribally specific names and roles for Two-Spirits and challenges the ways in which homophobia acts as a contemporary erasure, saying:

> The modern Indian has been programmed by white society so that his former mores and measurements have been changed to fit his ever-assimilating environment. With the loss of his religious rites and culture, there is probably no place for the contemporary *hee-man-he* [Cheyenne Two-Spirit] within that social structure. . . . Many traditionalists have become racist and sexist, and are generally disquieted when among homosexuals. Hollywood, TV, and the church have had a heavy influence on the changing attitude of Indian thought.[8]

In this commentary, Kenny notes the shift in many nations' and traditional Native people's views of diversity in gender and sex roles. Thus, even as he takes pain to validate the existence of multiple gender traditions in American Indian nations, he simultaneously acknowledges the cultural shifts that have led to a repression of such knowledge within Indigenous communities. In this way, Kenny addresses how dominant and nondominant communities can work in tandem to create a sort of social amnesia about Two-Spirit roles and histories.

I would suggest that Kenny's critique has not yet been given the weight it deserves in the history of Two-Spirit literature and criticism. Writing just a few years after Wounded Knee II and less than ten years after the Stonewall Rebellion, Kenny's essay represents an important early contribution to the field and a significant commentary on the shifting attitudes toward Two-Spirit people in the 1970s. By refuting dominant versions of queerness that often erased cultural difference to privilege sexuality and gender differences during this period, Kenny is able to offer an important social critique. He honors Mohawk and pantribal affiliations in his work while at the same time invoking Two-Spirit histories, thereby demonstrating that one need not choose between tribal ties and sexual / gender affiliation.

Additionally, he brings to light the fact that the problems of homophobia are not confined to dominant culture and suggests that negative attitudes toward nondominant sex / gender roles are part and parcel of assimilation. The latter claim functions as a rather radical slap in the face to those who, as a result of just the sort of social amnesia discussed earlier, would claim that *homosexuality*, rather than homophobia, is the product of assimilation. Thus, at a time when the hypermasculinized warrior ethos reigned supreme in representations of the American Indian Movement and white was still right for the vast majority of the gay rights movement, Kenny spoke of complex and longstanding traditions in American Indian communities to create a space for Two-Spirit people who fit in neither of those often limited and limiting categories.

Kenny's poem, "Winkte," can be read as the literary companion to the scholarly work of "Tinseled Bucks." In "Tinseled Bucks," Kenny quotes John Lame Deer as saying that Winkte have "'the gift of prophecy'"; they can "'give a newborn child a secret name . . . [that] is supposed to bring the bearer luck and long life."[9] In his poem, Kenny takes up these ideas and expands them, using the Lakota title, probably the best-known tribally specific appellation for a Two-Spirit person, as a metaphor for the larger body of diverse gender traditions that cross tribal boundaries.

Kenny begins the poem with an exclamation that sets the inclusive and laudatory tone of the piece: "We were special to the Sioux!" This exclamation works on two levels: First, it sets the stage for Kenny's reclamation of the accepted and often respected place Two-Spirit people historically held within their various tribal groups; and second, it situates the narrator as part of a collective body through the use of the plural pronoun "we." The construction of a collective is a particularly useful narrative move as it belies the rhetoric of "deviance" that situates any individual who falls outside a dominant heteropatriarchal hierarchy as dangerous outlier. The rhetoric of deviance, which ties queerness to danger and cultural corruption, can, at times, be difficult to combat in Indigenous communities, where cultural practices have been besieged by the pressures of assimilation. Kenny's "we," which he repeats throughout the piece (e.g., "to the Cheyenne we were no curiosity!"; "We were friends or wives of brave warriors"; "we were accepted into the fur robes," etc.) refutes the suggestion that Two-Spirit people were anomalies by continually situating them not simply as a defined group, but as multiple groups of people who were cherished by their individual nations.[10]

Ultimately, Kenny uses poetry as pedagogy, teaching readers Two-Spirit history by evoking specific tribal nations that had multiple gender traditions—the Sioux, Crow, Cheyenne, and Ponca—and listing a number of possible positions for Two-Spirit people within their various nations, calling them "friends," "wives," "warriors," healers, and holy men. Through this list, Kenny introduces readers to the tribal differences that historically existed between and among Two-Spirit roles in various Native nations. This litany of roles also implies that contemporary versions of homophobia were absent from such traditional settings because, along with listing the roles that *were* present, the narrator also notes the attitudes that *were not* present in each scenario. In the first stanza, for example, the speaker states that the Sioux "paid us with horses not derision," marking the role of the Winkte as one of cultural and economic value and implicitly condemning those who might, at the time of the poem's 1976 publication, greet Two-Spirits with Christian condemnation. This trend continues in stanza 2, which begins "To the Cheyenne we were no curiosity!" and recurs in stanza 4: "We were special to the Sioux, Cheyenne, Ponca / And the Crow who valued our worth and did not spit / Names at out lifted skirts nor kicked our nakedness."[11] Consequently, Kenny's layered commentary uses history as a way to undermine harmful attitudes toward contemporary queer Native people by invoking both acceptance and coalition.

One of the last and most interesting moves Kenny makes in this groundbreaking poem is to state that Two-Spirit people reinforce and strengthen, rather than threaten, Indigenous nationhood. In this way, the piece is very much in line with late twentieth and early twenty-first century Two-Spirit/LGBTQ creative writing and criticism in which authors like Craig Womack (Muscogee Creek/Cherokee), Deborah Miranda (Esselen/Chumash), and Qwo-Li Driskill (Cherokee) show how constructions of nationhood and queerness coalesce in Indigenous cosmologies. In "Winkte," this emphasis can be seen in Kenny's repetitive use of the metaphor of power. Initially, Kenny's speaker states that the Sioux respected the Winkte's "strange powers," which as I noted earlier, gave Two-Spirit people cultural capitol within the nation. This idea is followed in the third stanza with an emphasis on what Two-Spirit people give back to their nations. According to the narrator, some Two-Spirit people who experienced visions, saw "colors and design . . . on clouds," or heard "words [fall] from the eagle's wing." Those who were blessed in this way "took to the medicine tent, / And in their holiness made power / For the people of the Cheyenne Nation."[12] The "power" imagined by Kenny's speaker shifts the poem's focus from the idea of simple inclusion—the classic "seat at the table" rhetoric—to a more encompassing sense of tribal empowerment. In this logic, it is not only the Two-Spirit individual who stands to gain through a return to traditional recognition of Two-Spirit peoples and roles, but also the national collective. Two-Spirit people, Kenny argues, strengthen their tribal nations.

Again, I pause here to note the significance of Kenny's commentary, which even as the first published piece of contemporary Two-Spirit literature, contains surprisingly sophisticated nationalist arguments. Qwo-Li

Driskill notes the impact of this type of intervention in an essay entitled "Shaking Our Shells." While Driskill is speaking explicitly to other contemporary Cherokee Two-Spirit people, I believe hir claims address the influence work like Kenny's can have:

> the more central argument that [Two-Spirit people] are making is that our lives and identities—including, but not limited to issues of sexuality and gender—are integral to Indigenous struggles for decolonization, self-determination, and cultural continuance. Taking this stance isn't a "mainstreaming" tactic, but instead is a radical act against colonial mindsets and empires that surround us, trying to dissolve our claim on these continents. Two-Spirit people are not asking our tribal communities to accept us as "just like" straight gendered people. We are asking our communities to remember who we, as nations, are. And, just as importantly, we are asking our communities to imagine who we want to be. Two-Spirit people can change patterns in our communities that are damaging. We are looking to our core values to imagine the places we should have in our communities. Two-Spirit Cherokees are calling each other out of shadows to participate in the rebalancing of the world. And it is through living up to our responsibilities as Cherokees, particularly as Two-Spirits, that we "shell shake." We are insisting that we have a place in the circle and that our lives and work in the world is absolutely and uncompromisingly necessary to the continuance of Cherokee traditions.[13]

As Kenny does in "Winkte," Driskill, writing thirty years later, speaks of the power inherent in Two-Spirit involvement in their Indigenous nations. Kenny's poetry and essay are important early steps toward such goals taken at a moment in history when both queer and Indigenous political movements had only recently found their way into the pages of the national press.

Although these 1970s pieces are important, Kenny's work from the late 1970s to the present focuses primarily on the voices of the land, animals, and people of the Mohawk nation. Critically acclaimed texts like the historical poetry of *Blackrobe: Issac Jogues* (1982) and *Tekonwatonti: Molly Brant* (1992) tell first-person stories of the colonizers and leaders of the nation while gorgeous collections like *North: Poems of Home* (1977) or *Is Summer This Bear* (1985) give voice to the people and animals that inhabit Akwesasne Territory where "stone spruce / glisten on moon meadows / of north country."[14] Even texts that initially seem to focus elsewhere, like the elegiac *Mama Poems* (1984), which won the American Book Award, or the vivid poetry and explication of a collection like *Greyhounding This America*

(1988), have as their backdrop Kenny's memories and experiences in the Akwesasne community. But while not the most prevalent of his themes, Kenny's ruminations on sexuality, desire, and love are still well represented in the body of his work and are, as with the two earliest pieces I have analyzed, well worth further study because they have not yet been examined in the body of criticism on Kenny's work.

HUMOR, HISTORY, AND NATION IN *ONLY AS FAR AS BROOKLYN*

The collection in which Kenny delves most often into same-sex desire is *Only as Far as Brooklyn*, which was published in 1979 by Good Gay Poets publishing house, a press that came into being in 1972 with the rise of gay publishing in the United States that followed Stonewall.[15] Given that the press would in some way influence marketing, it is interesting that *Only as Far as Brooklyn* opens with the poem entitled "Boys." In many ways, this piece is classic Kenny with the evocation of landscape and Native tradition and especially the existence of a hawk, a recurring figure in Kenny's texts. Kenny notes in *On Second Thought* that as a young man he often "observed the flight of birds, especially the red-tailed hawk, which hunted the surrounding valleys and the woods of the hills." He goes on, while discussing how he rose out of a particularly dark period in his twenties, to discuss his affinity to a Robinson Jeffers poem "Hurt Hawks," saying "That had been me. I was a hawk."[16] This image of the hawk, which Kenny examines in some of his earliest work, is the primary metaphor in the first stanza of "Boys": "the hawk flew / to the crazy mountain / plums grew large and red / stained hands and teeth." The sensuality of the plums, which swell, darken, and mark the physical body, is met in stanza 2 by a sense of tumult: "the crazy mountain shivered / smoke rose from the rocks / the crazy mountain moved / called hawk, hawk / catch me in your talons."[17] This mélange of natural images can be read as a quintessential meditation on the environment; land is personified and images of the natural world are recounted and pondered by an unnamed and ungendered narrator. At the same time, however, "Boys" also can be interpreted as an erotic metaphor for desire (the swelling of the plums), physical contact (the "shive[ring], rising, and moving of the mountain), and abandon (the mountain's cry for physical connection with the hawk). The third stanza dispels this tension by situating the previous events as dream or vision and abruptly shutting down the burgeoning metaphors of desire with a comical turn that deflates the previously lush rhetoric of the poem: "Red plums fell to the grass / the hawk told me to go home." Kenny concludes with an emphasis on tradition and storytelling when the narrator addresses the hawk directly, saying "I must remember this story / to tell the young boys / fishing in the creek."[18] Given the time in which this poem was first published, this concluding stanza could have very different connotations for different readers: Kenny's non-Native queer readers might see the "young boys" as future members of the gay community to be told about the power and beauty of same-sex desire, whereas Kenny's Native audiences might see this imperative to remember and retell the story of the hawk and the mountain as a classic invocation of the oral tradition.[19] In this opening piece in the collection, then, multiple readings coexist as desire and tradition coalesce for the various audiences of Kenny's poems.

As the collection continues, images love, sensuality, and same-sex desire abound. The unnamed speaker in the poem "Of Love" contemplates absence and loss, deciding that "for a while / I shall not write of love" while another speaker, in the poem "Prison," considers the death of Walt Whitman's love, saying "Whitman . . . / loved a common soldier . . . / when he could only wipe the dying boy's sweat."[20] Kenny also republishes "Winkte" among these pieces and, at the same time, examines a less laudatory side of same-sex desire in poems like "Santa Fe, New Mexico," which offers a tongue-in-cheek examination of the potential political ramifications of anonymous sex in the "[u]nderground / toilet" of a "plush / hotel." Here young Yaqui and Navajo men cruise the stalls in "the only place / in town / where an Indian / can touch / an Irishman / with a western / accent / and keep / his Sacred / Mountains."[21] In a theme noticeably absent from his earlier work, Kenny deftly uses humor and same-sex desire to simultaneously critique colonialism, tourism, and contemporary Indian–White relations.

Although there are numerous topics for the poems in *Only as Far as Brooklyn*, two themes in particular stand out when the collection is examined as a whole. The first of these is an emphasis on Two-Spirit identity, where specific references to tribal affiliation are paired with sexuality in what are largely positive images of desire; the second of these themes is an examination of the darker side of gay male life in the 1970s when desire often melds with desperation in the late-night darkness of parks and alleys.[22] For the sake of space and continuity of focus, I concentrate on the first theme in this chapter. The emphasis on positive representations of Two-Spirit identity begin with "Winkte," which, as the fourth poem in the collection, functions here as a pedagogical tool, introducing unfamiliar readers to the history of Two-Spirit people in American Indian life. That grounding narrative then serves as a backdrop for Kenny's move to poems like "Apache," "Papago I," "Papago II," "Yuchi Brave," "Comanche of the Yamaha," and "United." Although each poem tells a different story, their narrative arc creates a story cycle in which tribal identity and same-sex desire come together in a series of positive representations of queer Native men. Thus, if "Winkte" provides grounding roles or categories, then the poems that follow offer snapshots of particular moments in the lives of male-bodied Two-Spirit Native people.

As the first example of one of these snapshots, "Apache" is a tender poem of an Oakland encounter between an "Apache warrior" and a "Mohawk." "In a night of smoke" the speaker observes the title character, who on this night is "safe from reservation / eyes and rules" when "gentle fingers / [turn] back the sheets."[23] There is a clear sense of relief in the poem as the Apache, who the speaker calls a "warrior of braids" ". . . le[aves] apprehension / in the wicki-up," trading pleasure for his fear of observation. Through these brief references to the existence of rules and fears, the poem subtly acknowledges the regulating power of homophobia even while focusing primarily on the delicious nature of the two men's encounter. In *Becoming Two-Spirit*, Brian Joseph Gilley discusses the ways in which contemporary Two-Spirit people engage with such homophobic responses from their home communities, noting "While Two-Spirit men see their communities as potentially hostile places, they also look to their tribes with a feeling of pride. They are proud of where they are from and who their relatives are, which makes their sense of alienation all the more troubling to them."[24] The poem, then, depicts the encounter between the Apache and Mohawk men as a moment of respite from such a psychic split in which neither tribal identity nor same-sex desire need be repressed. Instead, the Apache's sexuality is defined by his tribal identity: his "mouth the color / of Arizona sunsets" and his "body . . . / more eager than slithering lizards / on desert rocks."[25] In these images, the landscape becomes a sensual descriptor when markers of indigeneity such as, in this case, "braids," a "wicki-up," and desert landscape, function as vibrant descriptors of same-sex desire. Thus, Kenny's poetry creates a space where tribal identity is written on the body through the grammar of Two-Spirit erotics.

"Papago I" and "Papago II" function in much the same way as "Apache," in that these poems use a rapid-fire blend of images often related to indigeneity to describe the intimate relationship between two Native people. I read these poems as having a Two-Spirit sensibility given their context in this book, but both the speaker and the Papago person to whom the poems address are unnamed and ungendered, which is often the case in Kenny's love poetry. As with "Apache," there are textual references that suggest the speaker here is some version of Kenny himself: The last lines in "Apache" speak of the "Apache who struck a coup on a Mohawk / and left the bed victorious"[26] while the speaker in "Papago I" notes that "secrets / are long between your Arizona rocks / and my old cedar woods of home."[27] In the latter poem, the speaker repeatedly invokes Indigenous history as a metaphor for desire, describing, for example, the "centuries" of "breath," "blood," and "flesh" that come together in the passion of the couple's interactions. References to "corn" and "Arizona rocks" meet "wolves," "swept winds," and "breaking sky colors" as the speaker imagines all that sie intended to do to / with hir love, concluding with "I meant to leave my arms in your arms / and take only the gift of our voice / whispering the motions of my blood, / the taut muscles of our race."[28] N. Scott Momaday's ideas of memory in the blood come to mind as Kenny beautifully entwines a sense of long-standing Indigenous histories with the more immediate meeting of flesh and desire.

As he did in "Santa Fe, New Mexico," Kenny again blends humor with his depictions of Two-Spirit desire in "Comanche of the Yamaha." The poem, in which the "Comanche scout" roars in on his motorbike "eager to war Oakland / hotels and smoky barrooms" rewrites the meaning of words like "coup" and "lance" as nearly every element—air, water, and earth—responds to the "volcanic passion" that "erupt[s]" on this tumultuous trip.[29] The mischievous sense of play in this scene is a striking contrast to the final poem in the series of pieces from *Only as Far as Brooklyn* that emphasize positive images of Two-Spirit identity. If "Winkte" is read as the entry point of this collection, serving as what I termed a "pedagogical tool, introducing unfamiliar readers to the history of Two-Spirit people in American Indian life," then Kenny's poem "United" serves to bring the text full circle, following poems of political critique, passion, and humor with a return to the roots of Two-Spirit traditions.

Composed of three stanzas, "United" begins with the union of an unnamed and ungendered couple who "Moon music moved . . . together," invoking the earth, "Nevada mountains," and "the high hills of Mohawk country."[30] Stanza 2 moves from the couple to focus instead on the shifts in tribal traditions that have changed the way Two-Spirit people are perceived in most contemporary Native communities. The narrator speaks of "old Medicine Men" who "prodded by priest and politician, / no longer wear robes" and then moves on to note that, at the same time, "boys" no longer "gather holy corn / nor are celebrated on the warpath / and taken in love by strong warriors."[31] Loss is evident in the language of the speaker who clearly laments the cultural shifts that have wrought change in religious traditions and suppressed the expression of multiple gender roles. In this way "United" resembles "Winkte" (with which it was paired when later printed in *Living the Spirit*), because each poem refers to the historical acceptance of same-sex desire in American Indian nations. Whereas "Winkte" uses this history to call for a return to these earlier and, ironically, more forward-thinking tribal cosmologies, "United" ultimately suggests that such traditions are not lost but instead are temporarily suppressed. For although the "Medicine Men" and "boys" have changed the outward performance of their roles, the speaker claims "they remain in lodges and languages / where the vision is honored, / and grandfathers know nations will gather." Thus, "United" maintains that Two-Spirit roles and memories still exist in the spaces where cultural traditions and national identity are most honored.[32] Stanza 3 applies these ideas to the couple of the first stanza and the poem concludes as their relationship is reframed in light of Two-Spirit traditions: "Music moved them together; / breechclouts left at the door, / straight firs . . . ponderosa to cedar . . . / The first frenzied dance finished. / Wovoka shook hands with Cornplanter. / Earth parts for the seed of their firs."[33] The blending of the tree metaphors with the historical references to significant American Indian historical figures such as Wovoka, the Paiute prophet of the 1890 Ghost Dance, and the Seneca leader Cornplanter is quintessentially Kenny, showing that his focus on Two-Spirit traditions remains in line with the rest of his written work. More importantly, though, Kenny's work in "United" looks to the present and future of Two-Spirit people rather than simply evoking a romantic past. As a whole collection, then, *Only as Far as Brooklyn* takes readers through a long wild ride of desire that is by turns humorous and touching, and as seen in the bookends of "Winkte" and "United," also is a call for Two-Spirit desire to be recognized as an essential part of the fabric of American Indian nations and identities.

COMING TOGETHER: DANCING BACK STRONG THE NATION

For more than fifty years Kenny has been producing powerful poetry, essays, and fiction that has influenced several generations of readers and writers. As I noted in my introduction, the critical analysis of Kenny to this point has primarily focused on his historical poetry, his depictions of nature, and his integration of Mohawk cultural references into both of these themes. Although these ideas are important, a study of the ways in which Kenny employs metaphors of desire is long overdue. I have focused here on Kenny's Two-Spirit work, but there is much yet to be said about the implied pedophiliac desire in *Blackrobe: Issac Jogues* and the fascinating depictions of heterosexual desire in *Tetonwatonti: Molly Brant*. Such ideas have been mentioned in passing by critics like Patrick Barron and addressed briefly in Craig Womack's excellent review essay of *Tetonwatonti*, "The Spirit of Independence," but much still remains to be studied. Additionally, the first section of Kenny's recently released collection, *Connotations*, entitled "Part I: Lines on Canvas," fits well into such a study as nearly all the poems in the section ruminate on the relationships of male artists and their queer lovers and subjects. Perhaps E. Grant says it best when, speaking of *Tetonwatonti*, she noted to Kenny in a 1995 interview: "There's a lot of sex." In response, Kenny referred to a conversation with Paula Gunn Allen in which she told him:

> "You're the only one who's got the blood and guts and will stand up and use words like ['blood' or 'tomahawk']. . . . But you do it, and that's one of the original things you've done, to bring that back. Also, your sexual references," she said. "You have a lot of them even though we know Indians don't have sex." Well, they may do it through rape. (Laughter.) They don't love. We don't love. (More laughter.)[34]

Amidst the laughter, Allen makes an astute observation about the power of Kenny's writing: Kenny's ground-breaking depictions of Indigenous sexuality confront stereotypes of Indian stoicism and of the asexual squaw / Noble Savage or the hypersexualized Indian Savage, dispelling them with honest representations of desire. As part of this body of work, Kenny's depictions of Two-Spirit desire are exceedingly important. Although these images, on one hand, should be marked for their bravery as should all first steps in a new direction, I believe they are more significant for the way they unapologetically write Two-Spirit desire back into the social geography of tribal life. Thus, as my essay title suggests, Kenny's Two-Spirit images, to use his words, "dance back strong the nation" by dispelling the social amnesia that has denied the existence of Two-Spirit histories and attempted to erase the lives and literature of contemporary Two-Spirit people.

ACKNOWLEDGMENT

I thank Maria Calhoun, my research assistant in Kansas State University's Summer Undergraduate Research Opportunity Program, whose help on this chapter was absolutely invaluable. I could not have begun to compile and review the entire body of Kenny's work without her hard work and sharp insight.

NOTES

1. Kenny identifies *Dead Letters Sent* as his first book in the memoir that opens *On Second Thought* (19) and the text is most commonly cited as his first book. He did, however, print an earlier collection: in 1956, *The Hopeless Kill and Other Poems* was "published privately at the *Watertown Daily Times*—in the wee hours, in the dark upstairs rooms of what was then the paper's office on Stone Street" (33).

2. Roscoe, Will. "Native North American Literature," in *The Gay and Lesbian Literary Heritage* (New York: Henry Holt, 1995), 514–515.

3. Although I use "Two-Spirit" throughout this chapter, the term was not in common currency when Kenny published these first pieces. "Two-Spirit" was coined at a 1990 Winnepeg meeting as a way to (a) consciously resist the history of colonization and homophobia tied to "berdache," the derogatory term non-Native

anthropologists and missionaries historically used to refer to Indigenous people whose sexualities did not fit the dominant heterosexual binary; and (b) recognize and mark the distinct difference between indigenous and dominant histories of sexuality and gender constructions (Jacobs et al. 2).

I use Two-Spirit and Queer interchangeably throughout my work as the flexible boundaries of Queer identity allow for the multiple gender, sexuality, and occupation choices that would have historically fallen under the term Two-Spirit. Clearly, neither term is perfect. As Two-Spirit writer and activist Qwo-Li Driskill points out, "we need to remember that gender systems before invasion and colonization were not the same as they are now. While we subsume same-sex relationships and gender 'non-conformity' under the umbrella of 'Two-Spirit,' it is difficult to say if these identities were linked together in the past. There are numerous experiences and identities that we shove under terms like 'Two-Spirit' or 'Queer' or 'GLBT.' I've heard several different terms to talk about these identities in Cherokee, but I am going to use 'Two-Spirit' as my umbrella term here, knowing that not all of us use this term for ourselves any more than all of us use any of the other terms available to us in English. All of these terms and ideas are slippery and complicated, but 'Two-Spirit' carries with it a particular commitment to decolonization and Indigenous histories and identities that is at the center of this particular telling" ("Shaking" 125).

4. Kenny, Maurice, *On Second Thought: A Compilation*, edited by Gerald Vizenor and Louis Owens (Norman: University of Oklahoma Press, 1995), 58.

5. Ibid., 59.

6. Ibid., 59.

7. Kenny, *Living the Spirit*, 15.

8. Kenny, *Living the Spirit*, 28.

9. Kenny, *Living the Spirit*, 29.

10. Kenny, Maurice, "Winkte," in *Living the Spirit: A Gay American Indian Anthology*, Gay American Indians and Will Roscoe, eds. (New York: St. Martin's, 1988),153–154: 5, 6, 22, 6.

11. Ibid., 153: 5, 28–30.

12. Ibid., 153: 14, 15, 16–18.

13. Driskill, Qwo-Li, "Shaking Our Shells: Cherokee Two-Spirits Rebalancing the World," in *Beyond Masculinities: Essays by Queer Men on Gender & Politics*, Trevor Hoppe, ed. <http://www.beyondmasculinity.com>: 126.

14. Kenny, Maurice, *North: Poems of Home* (Marvin, SD: The Blue Cloud Quarterly, 1977), "Heavy Winter," 1–3.

15. Woods, Gregory, *A History of Gay Literature: The Male Tradition* (New Haven, CT: Yale UP, 1998), 10–11.

16. Kenny, Maurice, *On Second Thought: A Compilation*, edited by Gerald Vizenor and Louis Owens (Norman: University of Oklahoma Press, 1995), 18.

17. Ibid., 18:1–4, 5–8.

18. Ibid., 18:9–10, 14–16.

19. I do not mean to construct some sort of essential reader where one is queer *or* Native and where that identity necessarily drives reading practices. Actual readers would undoubtedly interpret Kenny's work in varying ways depending on their own knowledge base and their individual beliefs and reading practices.

20. Ibid., "Of Love," 9, 12.

21. Ibid., 14.

22. The poems I place in this second cycle are "Greta Garbo" (19), "Delusion" (26), "In Whitman Close" (27), and "No Name" (32).

23. Ibid., "Apache," 17.

24. Gilley, Brian Joseph, *Becoming Two-Spirit: Gay Identity and Social Acceptance in Indian Country* (Lincoln: University of Nebraska Press, 2006): 72.

25. Kenny, "Apache," 17.

26. Ibid., 17.

27. Kenny, *On Second Thought*, 20.

28. Ibid., 20.

29. Ibid., 37.

30. Ibid., 41. The dedication of this poem, "For Randy" and the references to "Nevada mountains" and the Paiute prophet Wovoka suggest that "United" may well be written for Randy Burns, who, as I noted in my text, cofounded the GAI.

31. Ibid., 41.

32. This claim is reminiscent of the intersections of memory, history, and desire depicted in "Papago I" and "Papago II."

33. Ibid., 41.

34. Grant, Elizabeth, "He Walks in Two Worlds: A Visit with Maurice Kenny," *Studies in American Indian Literatures* 7 no. 3 (1995): 21.

APPENDIX

MAURICE KENNY'S MOLLY BRANT

From Poetry to Play

Alan Steinberg

That Molly Brant was an historical woman is not without interest or significance. As an historical woman, Molly was an important, although neglected, figure in the complicated colonial events that led to the creation of the United States. Although her "political" actions helped shape the destiny of the Iroquois, perhaps all Native Americans, they are not what give Molly her literary or imaginative power or importance. That she was a beautiful woman, a wife and sister to important men, and a fierce warrior in her own right, makes her historical life especially interesting and complex. But, what finally makes Molly into an important literary figure is what Maurice Kenny imagines her knowing and feeling and saying and doing in each of these roles.

Thus, to "convert" Molly Brant from a poetry collection to a verse play seemed to me both logical and natural. Kenny's poetry always has been richly rhythmical and full of narrative and dramatic possibilities. As Joseph Bruchac has written, "A master lyricist, Kenny is also the creator of a new form of dramatic monologue in his recreations of the voices and the time of Isaac Jogues and Molly Brant." What I have mostly done is compress, confine, and embody. By bringing the characters together on stage, I have physically tried to dramatize the emotional tensions inherent in the original poems—give them a spatial dimension, as it were. Except for a handful of lines that serve mostly as explication or transition, all the speeches are drawn from the poems themselves, and the historical insertions are taken from the glossary and notes.

Structurally, the play is divided into three sections: *The Time Before, Molly and William*, and *The Time After*. The first part fuses both the historical and mythic early life of the Iroquois, the Native Peoples who inhabited the eastern lands before and during the coming of the Europeans, particularly the French and the British. The second section deals mainly with the lives of Sir William Johnson and Molly Brant. It details the tragically beautiful and bitterly ironic relationship between the Irish-born Willie, who became a British officer in charge of colonial Indian affairs and Tekonwatonti ("she who is outnumbered"), who, until Kenny's book of poems, was mostly remembered as the great Mohawk warrior Joseph Brant's sister. The final section recounts the sad and prophetic ending of this era—the death of Sir William, Molly and Joseph's ultimate defeat, and Molly's exile north with her eight children, where she is mostly forgotten by the British (and later the Canadians).

My sense was that these three realms of experience were vitally—and ironically—connected. Just as the Peacemaker struggled to forge a united confederation out of separate and often warring tribes, so Molly and William struggled to preserve a family relationship complicated by the hostilities around them and Johnson's own fierce ambitions and appetites—an Irishman serving the British with an African concubine and a German wife in addition to Molly and their eight children. These two struggles were themselves mirrored in the historical and political realm: the bloody conflict among the British, the French, and later, the Colonists for supremacy on the North American continent.

The "life" of Molly that Kenny has created naturally combines the mythic, the historical, the tragic, and, most of all, the enduring and the prophetic. The choices the Native peoples are forced to make in those chaotic years shape the destiny not only of the continent but the whole world, as it turns out. Hating and fearing the French and then the renegade Colonists even more than the British, Molly and her brother, Joseph, make the decision to ally with the British. Later, when the Colonists, aided by the French, defeat the British, Molly and Joseph and their followers are driven into exile in Canada—to be treated with neglect, if not the outright hostility they faced in the United States.

Through everything that happens, the Molly that Kenny creates remains true to herself. She loves but not blindly. William Johnson is a man of appetites, a man of prodigious energy in a world that demands audacity. His desire to have it all, combined with his intelligence and charisma, make him a formidable leader and lover—as well as a dramatic character. It is his ambition, his energy, his determination, and his cleverness that make him a match for Molly. Compared with the French and with the "rebel" Colonists, Sir William seems so much more attractive and consequential. Were he less so, Molly would not have loved him as much, committed herself to him so deeply. Perhaps, then, the history of the Native peoples might have been different.

Yet, Kenny's Molly Brant is herself sufficiently intelligent and aware to understand the larger context. Even as she leaves to go into exile in Canada, Kenny imagines Molly speaking to the victorious George Washington and asking not for sympathy or pardon, but reminding him, in the flush of his triumph, of the terrible costs of war: the dead and the dying on all sides; the destruction not only of people, but of animals and places and spirits—of Nature herself. Now, two hundred and fifty years later, with America once again at war, these words, as poetry and drama's best words always do, ring more prophetically true than ever.

As for the collaboration on the play, I think the Peacemaker himself would be pleased. I asked Kenny for permission to attempt the conversion, so that more people, particularly those not given to reading books of poetry, might get to know Molly. When the first draft was done I gave it to Kenny, saying something like "Tell me what you think isn't right or would embarrass Molly." He read it and told me. Another draft or two was done the same way—always with the intent of being true to the poems yet still seeking the compression that a one-act play demands.

Alan Steinberg

MAURICE KENNY'S *TEKONWATONTI / MOLLY BRANT*

A PLAY IN VOICES

Arranged by Alan Steinberg

Based on the book
Tekonwatonti / Molly Brant
By Maurice Kenny

White Pine Press
P.O. Box 236
Buffalo, New York 14201
ISBN: 1877727-20-2

Part One: The Time Before

Stage left behind a podium stands The Poet. Also on stage is The Drummer

(The Poet speaks / chants to the audience, accompanied by the Drummer as appropriate. As the characters / personae change, the Poet can assume these roles by use of minimal costuming—masks or symbols. More ambitiously, the characters can be played by separate actors who enter and then exit)

Water was first
Drop. Drop. Drop.
fog steamed
from mud

Legends began
Maguas. Mohaugs. Mohawks.
Drop. Drop. Drop.
Schoharie. Garoga. Canajoharie.
Drop. Drop.
And water creatures
turtle
bass, pike, trout, salmon,
sunfish, crawfish
Drop. Drop. Drop.

And the trees and flowers
white pine, reeds, elm, iris, maple
Drop. Drop.
And the animals
muskrat, beaver, otter

Birds swept across waters
down from the sky and clouds
loon rested on waves
eagle wheeled
and hawk
and common sparrow
Drop. Drop. Drop.

Feet touched the earth
on turtle's back
the great Tarachiawagon
and the giant shook
bear, wolf, turtle
raccoon, panther, deer
Drop. Drop. Drop.

Till at last
words echoed through the forest
under birch and poplar
sunning at the river edge
they came for venison
they came for fish
they came to clear the lands
to plant corn
and bean and squash
they came to thank sun and moon
stars and water
they came to thank the Creator
and to stay.

(If the Poet, then putting on a mask / symbol of peace)

I am the Peacemaker
Speak my tongue
Embrace my signs and sounds
Be the father of mighty peace
Allow the cub to create
Health and power
Through peace
Protect the spirit
Of the central fire
Of life.

Encourage men to gather.

Your lips are my mouth.

> **(removes the symbol of Peace / puts on symbol of War)**
> Among the Iroquois who hated all whites
> Among the whites who hated all Indians
> Hate was in the world
> And Hate must be remembered

(The French Jesuits were the Black Robes and so this character should be so costumed—even if only minimally)

I am Abbe Francois Picquet.
I will build a fort on Lake Ontario.

I will send the Mohawks to fight the British.
I will give them Christ and Rum.

Saving souls
Anointing heads
With sacred oils or waters
Blessing squaws on bended knees
Bringing brats to communion
Old men to benediction.

Not my purpose.

There are enough souls
In Paradise.

My purpose is to construct
A fort
Here on this muscled river

defy and defeat
the British lugs
that call themselves an army

skunks in rags with naked feet
caked in cow manure
and chicken turds

build a New France

and light heaven and earth

with scarlet bursts—
blood and fire

France
And the Black Robe Jesuits
Will rule
This new world

I pay for the scalps

Men or women
I pay for blood.

Now build, you scoundrels
Stone by stone.

Roll those boulders
Heave and sweat.

Hide your manhood
From your woman
With the breechclout
Still your carnal pleasure
Forget the hunt.

Time is of the utmost
Importance.
Hurry with those stones.
I see the light of dawn

Those southern savages
Will have our hair.

Now heave and pull
Carry stones

The flag of France
Must be raised

(the flag is raised—even if only a small one)

Behold!
My dream!

(if a separate actor, he exits, if the Poet, then a minimal costume change)

(enter if a separate actor, or if the Poet then a minimal costume change)

I am Clinton, George Clinton, First Governor of New York
And all I hear is Willie
Wanting this
Wanting that
Indians demanding more
More blankets
More iron pots
Germans hungry for Indian land

What can I advise the King?

I'll change my wig and powder it
That will be the end of it
For today

The French are at our rear
My wife with toothache

Oh, brush my sleeve
And be done with it.

How could I think
Indians
Would become
Too civilized for war?

(enter Young Molly)

I walk in fields
Fields that should have stalks
As high as my knees

But these young plants
Are dwarfed, pale rather
Than bright green
Leaves narrow and bent

What harvest will there be?

And beans. What of beans and squash?

First the French in black robes
Then the Hurons they brought.
Now the English redcoats camp
At the meadows edge
Following the Dutch.

Poisons have spilled into this earth
To water the seed kernels

We must bring the singers and the drum

(The Poet as Peacemaker, with a voice full of sorrow, downstage, soft drumming as appropriate)

Men have stomped
The ancient fire
Which I the Peacemaker have lit
With peace.

Men decrease. Women decrease. Children decrease.
Nations decrease.

(Lights down as the drumming ends)

End of Part One

Part Two: Molly and William

Again, the scenery and costuming can be minimal—symbolic or more realistic. What should be conveyed is how Sir William, of Irish birth, becomes a British officer and although married to a White woman, nevertheless was in love with Molly and was "married" to her in the traditional Mohawk way and dwelled with her as such and fathered many children by her.

(The Poet now assumes the role of presenter / explainer as first Molly and then Sir William appear on stage)

Poet (to the audience, as Molly as a young woman enters)
Tekonwatonti, known as Molly Brant, the Mohawk wife and then widow of Sir William Johnson, though Irish-born, a British General and later Baron, Superintendent of Iroquois affairs, and enlister of Mohawk warriors to fight for the British, was herself a mighty military commander. She controlled the Indian armies that, as allies of the British, fought the Whites decimating the Mohawk and Wyoming valleys. One word from her, wrote an officer officially in charge of His Majesty's Indian forces, goes further than a thousand words from any White man without exception.

Molly (to the audience)
I come from morning with light.
I come from river with song.
I come from the marsh with reeds.
I come out of the hills with cedar.
I come from woods with feathers.
I carry a fox skull
Red willow
Yarrow.

(said quietly but fiercely as she turns from audience to Sir William who enters, sits on a log or tree stump)
I go with fire.

(Molly, as appropriate, should actually or symbolically do what she describes)
I Tekonwatonti
Child of these rivers
Girl of this wood
Woman to be of this house
This bed of branches
Gathered for my husband
To be woman of this pot
Of mortar and pestle
Of fields of corn / brambles of berries
Of gathered sticks
To warm his thighs
Of breasts swollen with milk
For suckling children
And full of stories for winter nights

Pleased to love, happy to birth
Honored by a good man

(she moves from the place where she is doing these things to close to William who has been watching her, speaking now directly to him)

I take you into my house.
Place your club by my hoe near the door.
Lean your hunting bow beside them.
My grandfather is now your brother.

Here is bear fur for your sleep,
Corn and squash for your empty belly,
Hands to tend your needs, and children
To cover your bones when it is time.
Here is my name. You may keep it,
But never speak it to the listening winds.
Here is my morning and my night, my song . . .

Use them with gentle thoughts.

Together we will build tomorrow.

(William replies, touching her hair)

The tickle of your
Black hair
Tightens
The passion
Of my flushed cheek.

(Molly touches his hand with hers, then stands watching as William comes downstage to speak to the audience)

What more could a man ask . . .
Fields cleaned of rocks, a stout horse,
A warm cabin, a comely woman with strong hips
Holding a plate of roast venison in the doorway

Kingdoms are for kings
Victory and domination for generals
Spoils and rapine for malcontents.

Truly, do I thirst, tremble at the sight
Of unclaimed woods, woods which do not echo
The sounds of an ax striking bark; earth unplowed. . . .

And women, yes, oh yes, women!
The greatest gift of God.
Greater than breath itself.

Naked before me, before the reeds of the marsh,
The blossoms of the peach orchard, the flight
Of the crow; naked before the winds of time, before
Flesh sweet as the sweetest berry, as the sap
Of maples; naked before all eyes of the wood.

(he moves to where Molly is)

Ahhhhh! Woman, I'll round thy belly to a hundred sons.
Woman, and land: the earth is a fallow woman,
Its portals dark and mysterious . . .

(then moves back to address the audience again)

And if I have a German wife? ***(long pause)***
Should a man be content with a single field?

Kingdoms are for kings.

Am I a king? No.
Still . . . the moon is high
And full and sheds a prosperous light.

(he moves back to sit on his log again)

(Molly comes over to him, ministers to him, finally bending to rub his feet as she speaks the appropriate lines)

They believe I bewitched your Catherine
And her children of your loin.
They believe I have spelled my brother,
Joseph, so that he will wield a hatchet
Into their blonde heads.
They believe I can stop the wind,
Halt the rapids of the river,
Turn the sun into the moon, poison air.

I am a girl . . . waiting with a cup of tea,
Waiting in the cold bed across the long night.
I could not harm the mouse that steals your cheese,

Nor darn your sock lest you pain
From the bump of thread beneath your toe.

(William stands)

No more of this nonsense.
You are not a witch
But my little red berry
Under the sun, whose rays and the rain
Give sweetness to your fruit.

Go about your business:
Attend to your uncles, brother; pray
For me, and laugh in their faces.

(he turns to exit, pauses, turns back)

Keep the bedcovers warm.

(Molly speaks as if to the departed William and then more directly to the audience)

Tooth by tooth
I will gather wolf teeth
To hang about your throat.
They will give you strength
And bravery to meet the French.

One by one
I will yank tooth by tooth
From the dead wolf's jaw
As one by one you will have your men
Slay the French
And send their spirits back across the waters
With their Black Robes
Who kill the Wolf and Bear and Turtle
With disease under their skirts
Below that silver cross.

(she comes downstage, slowly opens her hand to reveal the wolf teeth)

See
See how these teeth sparkle
Under this first moon

(Molly exits. Sir William enters, speaks as if he can still see her, then more directly to the audience)

Molly, my dearest Molly. My simple child,
Consort and queen, general and wife
Concubine, friend and confidant
I speak the clichés
Of a schoolboy mesmerized by the moon.

(turning to the audience)

I am no Shakespeare nor orator.
Lobbyist that I am
I wield public words as though I owned language,
Command them to whatever service needed.

I forget you lead an army of warriors,
Forget you council chiefs and generals.
Would ride off to die as I would die
For these acres of woods and fields,
For the flag, for the crown.

(he moves to sit on the log again, suddenly weary, feeling old)

The mumblings of an aging man,
A foolish man who'd rather sleep with his head
In the folds of your loins than hold a crown upon
That head. You keep me young, Molly,
Keep the blood throbbing in veins which sag in the leg,
The liver forgetting to function as a liver should.

I feel it rotting, Molly, feel it crumble. If a heart cracks
Then surely the liver crumbles. One day I won't rise from the bed
But will lie back contented in our sweat, observe
Your march into chronicles. ***(pause, as he painfully rises, looks to where Molly exited)***
I do admit
To loving you.

(slight turn to the audience, as he begins to exit)

But now, well, war is waiting.

Lights Down

End of Part Two

Part Three: The Time After

(Molly enters. She is older, scarred by smallpox, stands behind an ornate wooden chair, a British parlor chair)

Artists have been here at the hall.
Paint from their pots
Has spilled and dotted the parlor rugs.
They painted William,
Ever so handsome,
And my brother Joseph, truly
Shining in his finest attire,
Red plumes, red cloak,
His sturdy neck tied
With the ribbon holding the white shell.

They asked for my pose.
I was flattered
That they would have this Indian
Woman sit for their brush.
One painter wanted me in silk,
The other, Oh, no
Sit here on this stone in the sunshine,
The woods and river behind,
In your war bonnet.
War bonnet, I questioned?
True I have ridden to war,
But I wore no feathers. Ridiculous.

(she moves closer downstage)
I held up the mirror
And instantly knew I could not sit,
I could never look at the reflection.

I did not wish my great-grandchildren to see
my face, to see the smallpox.

Oh, but we can erase those scars,
One painter exclaimed.
But could he, truly,
Could he really erase my scars
And the scars that still cling to the lodges
Of Canajoharie; replace
Living flesh on emptied beds, beds covered
With blankets soaked in the liquids of death?

It wasn't just my pitted face,
Scars' rivulets on my cheek,
Holes on my brow.
It was the terror, horror, pain
And the death of all the others.

No, not today I said graciously,
Appreciatively;
No, do not paint today;
Perhaps tomorrow.

And that is the reason
You will have no portrait of me.

(she sits wearily on the chair as the Poet leads an aged, infirm William across the stage, William speaking as if confused, delirious, as if oblivious to Molly)

Catty, Catty who?
My wife?
My wife is Molly, Brown Mary.

Oh! Yes, the servant girl
I bought those years back.
The German from the Flats.
Indentured.

Yes, she bedded in my bed.
Yes, I did take her to marry.
That long night she died

Yes, I placed a copper ring on her finger
And took the shame from her cheek.

The least I could do. Poor Catherine.

(as they continue across the stage and exit)

Bury the remains, her remains,
My beloved wife . . . Catty
Next to mine.

(he stops one last time, speaks as if it were to Molly)

Molly, oh Molly . . . forgive me.

(the Poet and William exit, then the Poet returns, speaks to the audience)

He gave up
The ghost
Mysteriously
Holding a council
Celebration with
A large group of Iroquois.
(pause, more intimate)
Willie succumbed to the cold
Embrace of death
July 11, 1774.

(Molly now rises, speaks in anguish)

Kwaaaaaaaaa

My hair streams in the river,
Chips of my flesh shrivel under the sun,
The nub of my little finger
Is buried in the earth with his bones.

Kwaaaaaaaaa

I have no arms to hold me
No cheek against my own

No might to protect my house
Or the limbs of my children.
Who will hunt for my pot?

Kwaaaaaaaaaaaaa

Eight times I gave him
The children of his flesh.
Twenty-one years we lay
Under the summer stars.
How do I pull grass over his face now?

Kwaaaaaaaaaaaaaaaaaaaaaaaaaaaaaa

(Molly comes downstage to address the audience)

If I could scratch figures
I would show you the fathers of Thirteen Fires
How my many grandfathers struggled
To construct the Longhouse
How you took up the wisdom
Of our great and wise Peacemaker
As you accepted our corn
Took trout from our rivers
Scalped hair from our heads.

May your fire burn
And allow our fire
To blaze as well,
Sign of spirit.
Symbol of survival,
Our cornfields,
Our white pine of peace
Eagle diligently watching
All the skies.

A people who do not remember:

Rain which falls upon a rock.

(she goes to sit beside the fire pit, stirs a pot as in the poem)

As women stir soup tonight
Children stand about the great pot
Holding bellies angry from war
Bellies angry no rabbit or deer
Was left by the British
Army in the woods for their fathers' arrows.

(again she moves downstage, but keeps looking back)

This cold night
Wind blowing, howling hard
Down from the Adirondacks
On the north, snow piling up
To the birch of this longhouse.
Across the snowfall I can see
The children at the pot
Of boiling moss, their only supper

(now speaking more directly to the audience)

If William were here,
If William were here
He would demand these stingy
Untrusty redcoats at least
Kill one of their horses to feed
These children,
These children who will rise up
Thin warriors without meat on their bones
A bowl of dried corn
Some sweet maple . . . oh William
Where are the sons you promised.

(pause, solemn)

The rebels will win, and we lose,
Not the redcoats, we, we the people,
The "real people" will lose.

Oh, Willie, I need your guidance
Whisper the message of your knowledge.
Behind me,

The warriors,
Young and fearless,
Handsome in their war paint,
Proud in stance.

I, too, am proud
To lead them
To battle, victory–
Perhaps death.

In death their blood
Will scar my hands forever;
The tears of their women—
Mothers, wives, daughter–
Will ring in my ears.
The loss will be too great to bear.

Oh Willie
Give me good sense
So I may not waste
A single drop of the blood these young and brave
Who fight for England now
But truly for the survival
And strength of the Longhouse.

(Molly exits wearily)

(Poet enters and gives the brief history of the Outcome, then puts on Washington mask or symbol to become George Washington or if a separate actor, then Washington enters)

Nothing good remained.
There was, in 1776, the Declaration.
A year later, Joseph, her brother, was defeated
By General Herkimer near Oriskany.
Then, Joseph and Molly make war
On the Revolutionary Army
But are defeated
After which George Washington
Orders the destruction

Of all the Iroquois,
Man, Woman, and Child.

(Molly enters again, speaks as if to Washington)

I wish never to live to see
Another war
I've gagged on flesh
And choked on blood.
I've seen the bones of my brothers
Float in the river
Smelled the stench of their rot.
My arms are weary from the
Weight of rifles.
Villages burned to the ground,
Old men pierced on stockade posts.
Women and babies sleep
On the scars of bayonets.
Maggots infest the bed.

General George, town destroyer
You have won,
Won and accomplished more in your victory
Than you ever dreamed.

Our blood is your breakfast. . . .
Our stars are yours now
Our blood stains your flag.
Your hatred controls our destiny.

May your nation never know
This unbearable loss, this pain,
This exodus from home,
The smoking earth,
The sacred graves of the dead.

I go to bathe in the river to wash
Away the blood of war.

As your stars, General George, rise
Above the many battlegrounds

I want you to remember all those
Who died
So that your flag may wave
in tribute.

(The Poet speaks through the Washington mask or a separate actor)

The War is over.
Revolutionary bayonets
Will drive you from the river
Because of your husband's
British allegiance.
You will flee to Canada
Pulling your eight children
By their hair.

(The Poet or Washington slowly exits, as Molly speaks to the audience)

I left his dusting bones,
The impression of his death kiss,
His house to burn rafter by rafter.
I left the earth, the spring smell of the river,
Cornfields, larks which had sung
Me to afternoon sleep,
The flesh of woodchuck and deer,
Breath of hot panthers prowling
Mountains above the villages.
I left my sons' placentas in leaves
Tied with wild grapevines.
I left the voice and vision of my ancestry:
My father's echo, my mother's lullaby;
The yellow moon and stars rising
Over old hills and that village
Where Ayonwatha and the Peacemaker
Plotted the founding of the great
League of Five Nations.
I fled muskets, bayonets, terror,
And extermination as Benjamin Franklin
Had so often suggested.

Driven like a leper from my home,
A fugitive, a beggar

To a strange land where no lodge opened
To my children, nor to my brother bathed
In the blood of American soldiers.
I carried a small packet of soil,
Earth rich and dark in claim,
Moist from women's sweat
Working the fields of squash,
Still firm from feet dancing in celebration,
Warm with William's footprint.

I fled. My sons will hunt.
My daughters plant.
I will pull grass over my tired head.

(she moves downstage, speaks with great finality, certainty)

This I know.

As a deer warms my belly
We warm the earth

As I would suck the marrow of a bone
The earth has a right to mine.

Even the river one day
Must dry, become the sun,
The clouds again.

This I know.

And yet I mourn
My own flesh and yours
As we wither in winter
As we take our place in death
In earth
And become spring's new green corn
Autumn's apple
The calf my grandson shall one day
Feast upon.

The sun's cycle
The wind's return

The weeds and berries of the fields
Pine needles on the mountain slope
The trickle of the spring
Drop of the rain.

This I know.
It is natural
And as it should be.

(She turns to exit, stops, looks back)

The shell becomes the sand.
The sand the sea.

Exit

Lights Down

End of the Play

BIBLIOGRAPHY

SELECTED POETRY BY MAURICE KENNY

And Grieve, Lesbia. New York: Aardvark Press, 1960.

Between Two Rivers: Selected Poems, 1956–1984. Fredonia, NY: White Pine Press, 1987.

Blackrobe: Poems by Maurice Kenny. Saranac Lake, NY: North Country Community College Press, 1982.

Boston Tea Party. San Francisco: Soup Press, 1982.

Carving Hawk: New and Selected Poems, 1953–2000. Buffalo, NY: White Pine Press, 2002.

Connotations. Fredonia, NY: White Pine Press, 2008.

Dancing Back Strong the Nation: Poems by Maurice Kenny. 1979. Fredonia, NY: White Pine Press, 1981.

Dead Letters Sent, and Other Poems. New York: Troubadour Press, 1958.

Greyhounding This America: Poems and Dialog by Maurice Kenny. Chico, CA: Heilelberg Graphics, 1988.

Humors And/Or Not So Humorous. Buffalo, NY: Swift Kick Press, 1988.

I Am The Sun. 1973. Buffalo, NY: White Pine Press, 1979.

In the Time of the Present: New Poems by Maurice Kenny. East Lansing: Michigan State University Press, 2000.

Is Summer This Bear. Saranac Lake, NY: Chauncy Press, 1985.

Kneading the Blood. New York: Strawberry Press, 1981.

Last Mornings in Brooklyn: Poems by Maurice Kenny. Norman, OK: Point Riders Press, 1991.

North: Poems of Home. Marvin, SD: Blue Cloud Quarterly, 1977.

On Second Thought: A Compilation. Norman: University of Oklahoma Press, 1995.

Only as Far as Brooklyn. Boston: Good Gay Poets Press, 1979.

Tekonwatonti/Molly Brant (1735–1795): Poems of War. Fredonia, NY: White Pine Press, 1992.

The Hopeless Kill. Watertown, NY: Watertown Daily Times, 1956.

The Mama Poems. Buffalo, NY: White Pine Press, 1984.

The Short and the Long of It. Fayetteville: University of Arkansas Press, 1990.

The Smell of Slaughter. Marvin, SD: Blue Cloud Quarterly Press, 1982.

With Love to Lesbia. New York: Aardvark Press, 1959.

OTHER WORKS WRITTEN OR EDITED BY MAURICE KENNY

Kenny, Maurice. *Backward to Forward: Prose Pieces*. Fredonia, NY: White Pine Press, 1997.

———. *Rain and Other Fictions*. Fredonia, NY: White Pine Press, 1990.

———, ed. *Stories for a Winter's Night*. Minneapolis: Consortium Book Sales and Distribution, 1999.

———. *Tortured Skins and Other Fictions*. East Lansing: Michigan State University Press, 2000.

———, ed. *Wounds Beneath the Flesh: Fifteen Native American Poets*. Fredonia, NY: White Pine Press, 1995.

SELECTED INTERVIEWS AND AUTOBIOGRAPHICAL ESSAYS BY MAURICE KENNY

Grant, Elizabeth. "He Walks in Two Worlds: A Visit with Maurice Kenny," *Studies in American Indian Literature* 7 (1995): 17–24.

Kenny, Maurice. "Angry Rain: A Brief Autobiographical Memoir from Boyhood to College." *Contemporary Authors Autobiography Series* 22 (1995): 121–72.

———, "Introduction: A Memoir" in *On Second Thought: A Compilation*. Norman and London: University of Oklahoma Press, 1995, 1–63.

———. "Our Own Pasts: An Interview with Maurice Kenny." In *Survival This Way: Interviews With Native American Poets*, edited by Joseph Bruchac, 145–55. Tucson: University of Arizona Press, 1987.

———. Interview by Susan Ward. 28 October 2002.

———. "Prelude" to *Between Two Rivers: Selected Poems 1965–1984*. Fredonia, NY: White Pine Press, 1987, 1–5.

———. "Tremolo" in *Backward to Forward: Prose Pieces*. Fredonia, NY: White Pine Press, 1997, 159–70.

———. "Waiting at the Edge." In *I Tell You Now: Autobiographical Essays by Native American Writers*, edited by Brian Swann and Arnold Krupat, 37–54. Lincoln and London: University of Nebraska Press, 1987.

Nowak, Mark. "Historian of Home: A Talk with Maurice Kenny." *River City Press*. 1997.

Sweeny, Chad. "An Interview with Maurice Kenny," *World Literature Today:A Literary Quarterly of the University of Oklahoma* 79 (May–Aug 2005): 66–69.

SELECTED CRITICAL WORKS ON MAURICE KENNY

"ASAIL Bilbiography, no. 4: Maurice Kenny." *Studies in American Indian Literature* 7 (Winter 1983): 1–7.

Barron, Patrick. "Maurice Kenny's *Tekonwatonti, Molly Brant*: Poetic Memory and History." *MELUS* 25 (2000): 31–64.

Bruchac, Joseph. "New Voices from the Longhouse: Some Contemporary Iroquois Writers and their Relationship to the Tradition of the Ho-de-no-sau-nee." In

Coyote Was Here: Essays on Contemporary Native American Literary History and Political Mobilization, edited by Bo Scholer, 147–61. Arhus, Denmark: Seklos, 1984.

Fast, Robin Riley. ""Resistant History: Revisiting the Captivity Narrrative in 'Captivity' and Black Robe: Isaac Jogues." *American Indian Culture and Research Journal* 23, no. 1 (1999): 69–86.

Gross, Judith. "Molly Brant: Textual Representations as Cultural Midwifery." *American Studies* 40, no. 1 (1999): 23–40.

Kelsey, Penelope Myrtle. "Tribal Theory Travels: Kanien'kehaka Poet Maurice Kenny and the Gantowisas." In *Tribal Theory in Native American Literature: Dakota and Haudenosaunee Writing and Worldviews*. Lincoln: University of Nebraska Press, 2008. 112–129.

Ruppert, James. "The Uses of Oral Tradition in Six Contemporary Native American Poets." *American Indian Cultural and Research Journal* 4 (1980): 87–10.

Scott, Carolyn D, "Baskets of Sweetgrass: Maurice Kenny's *Dancing Back Strong the Nation* and *I Am the Sun*." *Studies in American Indian Literature* 7 (Winter 1983): 8–13.

Schweninger, Lee. "To Name Is to Claim, or Remembering Place: Native American Writers Reclaim the Northeast." In *Coming into Contact: Explorations in Ecocritical Theory and Practice*, edited by Annie Merrill Ingram, Ian Marshall, Daniel J. Philippon, and Adam W. Sweeting, 76–92. Athens: University of Georgia Press, 2007.

Womack, Craig S. "The Spirit of Independence: Maurice Kenny's Tekonwatonti. Molly Brant: Poems of War." American Indian Cultural and Research Journal 18 (1994): 95–118.

SELECTED CRITICAL WORKS ON NATIVE AMERICAN LITERATURE

Allen, Paula Gunn. *The Sacred Hoop: Recovering the Feminine in American Indian Traditions*. Boston: Beacon, 1992.

———. "A Stranger in my Own Life: Alienation in Native American Prose and Poetry." *ASAIl Newsletter* 3, no. 1 (Winter, 1979). 7 September 2007, <http://oncampus.richmond.edu/faculty/ASAIL/SAILns/31.html.

Arquette, Mary. "The Animals." *Words that Come Before All Else: Environmental Philosophies of the Haudenosaunee*, edited by Haudenosaunee Environmental Task Force, 82–101. Akwesasne: North American Indian Traveling College, 1999.

Awiakta, Marilou. *Selu: Seeking the Corn-Mother's Wisdom*. Golden, CO: Fulcrum, 1993.

Barron, Patrick. "Maurice Kenny's *Tekonwatonti/Molly Brant*: Poetic Memory and History," *MELUS* 25, no. 3/4 (Fall/Winter 2000), 31–64.

Benedict, S. "For Our Mother Earth Iethi'nistenha Onhwenstia." *Words that Come Before All Else: Environmental Philosophies of the Haudenosaunee*, edited by Haudenosaunee Environmental Task Force, 15–24. Akwesasne: North American Indian Traveling College, 1999.

Bevis, William. "Native American Novels: Homing In." In *Recovering the Word: Essays on Native American Literature*, edited by Brian Swann and Arnold Krupat, 580–618. Berkeley, CA: University of California Press, 1987.

Brooks, Lisa. *The Common Pot: The Recovery of Native Space in the Northeast*. Minneapolis: University of Minnesota Press, 2008.

Calloway, Colin G. *The American Revolution in Indian Country: Crisis and Diversity in Native Americans Communities*. Cambridge, England and New York: Cambridge University Press, 1995.

Cook, Katsi Iewirokwas. "The Berries." In *Words that Come Before All Else: Environmental Philosophies of the Haudenosaunee*, edited by Haudenosaunee Environmental Task Force, 64–68. Akwesasne: North American Indian Traveling College, 1999.

Cornplanter, J. J. *Legends of the Longhouse*. 1938. Ohsweken: Iroqrafts, Ltd., 1992.

De Certeau, Michel. *The Practice of Everyday Life*. Berkeley: University of California, 2002.

Driskill, Qwo-Li. "Shaking Our Shells: Cherokee Two-Spirits Rebalancing the World." *Beyond Masculinities: Essays by Queer Men on Gender & Politics*. In Trevor Hoppe, ed. <http: // www.beyondmasculinity.com>: 120–34.

———. *Walking with Ghosts*. Cambridge, England: Salt Publishing, 2005.

———. "Stolen From Our Bodies: First Nations Two-Spirits/Queers and the Journey to a Sovereign Erotic." *Studies in American Indian Literature* 16, no. 2 (Spring 2004): 50–64.

"Environment," *The Great Peace: the Gathering of the Good Minds* [CD-ROM]. Brantford, Ontario: Working World Media, 1998.

Feister, Lois M., and Bonnie Pulis. "Molly Brant: Her Domestic and Political Roles in Eighteenth-Century New York." In *Northeastern Indian Lives, 1632–1816*, edited by Robert Steven Grumet, 295–320. Amherst: University of Massachusetts Press, 1996.

George-Kanentiio, Doug. *Iroquois Culture & Commentary*. Santa Fe, NM: Clear Light Publishers, 2000.

Gilley, Brian Joseph. *Becoming Two-Spirit: Gay Identity and Social Acceptance in Indian Country*. Lincoln: University of Nebraska Press, 2006.

Graymont, Barbara. *The Iroquois in the American Revolution*. Syracuse, NY: Syracuse University Press, 1972.

———. "Konwatsi?tsianiénni" in *Dictionary of Canadian Biography*, © 2000 University of Toronto/Université Laval. http: // www.biographi.ca/EN/ShowBio.asp?BioId=36113&query=molly%20AN%20brant.

Green, Gretchen "Molly Brant, Catharine Brant, and Their Daughters: A Study in Colonial Acculturation." *Ontario History*, LXXXI, no. 3 (September 1989), 235–50.

Greer, Allan, ed. *The Jesuit Relations*. New York: Bedford/St. Martin's, 2000.

Haas, Angela. "Wampum as Hypertext: Re-visioning the History of Hypertext Theory and Re-imagining the Future of Hypertext Studies." *Studies in American Indian Literatures* 19, no. 4 (2007): 77–100.

Harjo, Joy. "New Orleans." In *Songs from this Earth on Turtle's Back*, edited by Joseph Bruchac 95–96. Greenfield Center, NY: Greenfield Review Press, 1983.

Heth, Charlotte. Ed. *Native American Dance: Ceremonies and Social Traditions*. Washington, DC: National Museum of the American Indian Smithsonian Institution, 1992.

Hewitt, J. N. B. and Jeremiah Curtin. *Seneca Fiction, Legends and Myths 1910–1911*. Part I. Bureau of Ethnology, 32nd Annual Report. Washington DC: US Government Printing Office, 1918.

———. *Seneca Fiction, Legends and Myths 1910–1911*. Part II. Bureau of Ethnology, 32nd Annual Report. Washington DC: US Government Printing Office, 1918.

Huey, Lois M., and Bonnie Pulis. *Molly Brant: A Legacy of Her Own*. Youngstown, New York: Old Fort Niagara Association.

Jacobs, Sue-Ellen, Wesley Thomas, and Sabine Lang, eds. *Two-Spirit People: Native American Gender Identity, Sexuality and Spirituality*. Urbana: University of Illinois Press, 1997.

Justice, Daniel. *Our Fire Survives the Storm: A Cherokee Literary History*. Minneapolis: University of Minnesota Press, 2006.

Karen L. Kilcup, ed. *Native American Women Writers, c. 1800–1924: An Anthology*. Malden, MA: Blackwell, 2000.

Krupat, Arnold. "American Histories, Native American Narratives." *Early American Literature* 30 (1995): 165–174.

Larkin, Joan and Carl Morse. *Gay and Lesbian Poetry in Our Time: An Anthology*. New York: St. Martins, 1988.

Lickers, F. Henry. "The Creator." In *Words that Come Before All Else: Environmental Philosophies of the Haudenosaunee*, edited by Haudenosaunee Environmental Task Force, 152–59. Akwesasne: North American Indian Traveling College, 1999.

Lyons, Oren. "Traditional Native Philosophies Relating to Aboriginal Rights." In *The Quest for Justice:Aboriginal Peoples and Aboriginal Rights*, edited by Menno Boldt. Toronto: University of Toronto Press, 1985.

Mann, Barbara. *Iroquois Women: The Gantowisas*. New York: Peter Lang, 2004.

Mohawk, John C. *Iroquois Creation Story: John Arthur Gibson and J.N.B. Hewitt's Myth of the Earth Grasper*. Buffalo: Mohawk Publications, 2005.

———, "Origins or Iroquois Political Thought." *New Voices From the Longhouse*, edited by Joseph Bruchac. Greenfield Center: The Greenfield Review Press, 1989.

Mt. Pleasant, Alyssa. "After the Whirlwind: Maintaining a Haudenosaunee Place at Buffalo Creek, 1780°–1825." PhD Dissertation, Cornell University, 2007.

———. "Searching for Her Rightful Place: Jigonsaseh's Legacy Amongst the Haudenosaunee," unpublished mss on file with author. Delivered as a paper at All Women of Red Nations: Weaving Connections (11th Annual Women's Studies Conference), Southern Connecticut State University, October 2001.

O'Brien, Jean M. "'Vanishing' Indians in Nineteenth-Century New England: Local Historians' Erasure of Still-Present Indian Peoples." In *New Perspectives on Native North America: Cultures, Histories, and Representations*, edited by Sergei A. Kan and Pauline Turner Strong,. Lincoln: University of Nebraska Press, 2006.

"Oneidas' Declaration of Neutrality . . . to the Four New England Colonies," *American Archives*, 1st ser., 4:116–7.

Ortiz, Simon. *From Sand Creek*. Tucson: University of Arizona Press, 1981.

Parker, Arthur C. and Harriet Maxwell Converse, eds. *Myths and Legends of the New York Iroquois*. Albany: The University of the State of New York, 1981.

Parker, Arthur C. "The Constitution of the Five Nations" In *Parker on the Iroquois*, edited by William Fenton. Syracuse: Syracuse University Press, 1968.

Patterson, Neil. "The Fish." In *Words that Come Before All Else: Environmental Philosophies of the Haudenosaunee*, Haudenosaunee Environmental Task Force, 44–50. Akwesasne: North American Indian Traveling College, 1999.

Powell, Malea D. "Down by the River, or How Susan La Flesche Picotte Can Teach us about Alliance as a Practice of Survivance." *College English* 67, no. 1. (2004): 38–60.

Roscoe, Will. "Native North American Literature." *The Gay and Lesbian Literary Heritage*. Henry Holt: New York, 1995. 514–15.

Savageau, Cheryl. *Mother/land*. Cambridge: Salt Publishing, 2006.

Sellers, Stephanie Anne. "Redefining Native American Autobiography: The Case of Tekonwatonti," PhD Dissertation, Union Institute, 2004.

Taylor, Diana. *The Archive and the Repertoire: Performing Cultural Memory in the Americas*. Durham, NC: Duke University Press, 2003.

Tehanatorens. "The Gift of the Great Spirit." *Tales of the Iroquois: Vols. I and II*. Ohsweken: Iroqrafts Ltd., 1992. 34–40.

Teuton, Christopher. "Theorizing American Indian Literature: Applying Oral Concepts to Written Traditions." *Reasoning Together: Native Critics Collective*, 209–14.Norman: University of Oklahoma Press, 2008.

Wagner, Sally Roesch. *Sisters in Spirit: Haudenosaunee (Iroquois) Influences on Early American Feminists*. Summertown, Tennessee: Book Publishing Company, 2001.

Warrior, Robert Allen. *Tribal Secrets: Recovering American Indian Intellectual Traditions*. Minneapolis: University of Minnesota, 1995.

Williams, Paul Kayanesenh. "Creation." In *Words that Come Before All Else: Environmental Philosophies of the Haudenosaunee*, edited by Haudenosaunee Environmental Task Force. Akwesasne: North American Indian Traveling College, 1999. 1–7.

Womack, Craig S. *Art as Performance, Story as Criticism*. Norman: University of Oklahoma Press, 2009.

———. *Drowning in Fire*. Tucson: University of Arizona Press, 2001.

———. "Howling at the Moon: the Queer but True Story of My Life as a Hank Williams Song." In *As We Are Now: Mixblood Essays on Race and Identity*, edited by William S. Penn, 28–49. Berkeley: University of California Press, 1997.

———. "Politicizing HIV in Indian Country." In *Native American Religious Identity: Unforgotten Gods*, edited by Jace Weaver, 199–216. Maryknoll, NY: Orbus Books, 1998.

———. "The Spirit of Independence: Maurice Kenny's Tekonwatonti/Molly Brant: Poems of War." *American Indian Culture and Research Journal* 18, no. 1 (1994): 95–118.

———. *Red on Red: Native American Literary Separatism*. Minneapolis: University of Minnesota Press, 1999.

Woods, Gregory. *A History of Gay Literature: The Male Tradition*. New Haven, CT: Yale University Press, 1998.

LIST OF CONTRIBUTORS

Lisa Brooks, an Abenaki writer and scholar, is Associate Professor of History and Literature and of Folklore and Mythology at Harvard University, where she teaches courses in Native American literature, history and oral traditions. Her book *The Common Pot: The Recovery of Native Space in the Northeast* (University of Minnesota Press) focuses on the role of writing as a tool of social reconstruction and land reclamation in the Native networks of the northeast.

Joseph Bruchac III is the author of over 120 books for adults and young readers, Joseph Bruchac's writing often draws on the Adirondack mountain region of New York State and his Abenaki Indian ancestry. He and his two grown sons, James and Jesse, work extensively in projects involving the preservation of Abenaki culture, language and traditional Native outdoor skills. (see <ndcenter.org>) A former varsity wrestler at Cornell University, he has been a martial arts teacher for more than thirty years, focussing in particular on the martial art of Indonesia, Pentjak silat in which he holds the rank of Master.

Nicholle Dragone is an Indigenous scholar of Dakota/Lakota descent who completed her dissertation, *Articulating the Foundations of the Indigenous Rights Movement as an Earth-Rights Based Indigenous Jurisprudence: A Textual Analysis*, in 2011 at SUNY Buffalo. Her recent scholarship explores the legal and narrative history of the International Indigenous Rights Movement as it relates to the historical roots and philosophical underpinnings of Indigenous Peoples' international environmental and ecological work. As a detailed study of the centrality of the Natural World and its rights to Indigenous diplomacy at the international level, Dragone's dissertation proposes that an international earth-rights based Indigenous jurisprudence is emerging out of Indigenous rights and environmental activism. Her MA Thesis, *Haudenosaunee Literature: A View From Outside the Culture*, which won the 2002 Wordcraft Circle of Native Writers Academic Writer of the Year Award, is currently being revised for publication.

Qwo-Li Driskill is a Cherokee (non-citizen) Two-Spirit/Queer activist, writer, and performer. S/he is the author of *Walking with Ghosts: Poems* and the co-editor of the collections *Queer Indigenous Studies: Critical Interventions in Theory, Politics, and Literature* and *Sovereign Erotics: A Collection of Two-Spirit Literature*, both published by University of Arizona. Qwo-Li is an assistant professor in the Department of English at Texas A&M University.

Eric Gansworth (Onondaga) is Lowery Writer-in-Residence at Canisius College in Buffalo, NY. His nine books include *Extra Indians* (American Book Award), and *Mending Skins* (PEN Oakland Award). Gansworth is also a visual artist. He has had solo visual art exhibits at Colgate University, Niagara University, Bright Hill Center, SUNY Oneonta, Westfield State University, among other art spaces. His collection of poems and paintings, *A Half-Life of Cardio-Pulmonary Functions*, was voted to the Number 3 position on the National Book Critics Circle's "Good Reads" List in 2008. His play, *Re-Creation Story*, was selected for the Public Theater's Native Theater Festival, in New York City Theater commissions include *Rabbit Dance* a one act and *Home Fires and Reservation Roads*, a multimedia performance piece, both of which were mounted in full productions during 2011. His written work has appeared in *Kenyon Review*, *Boston Review*, *Shenandoah*, *Poetry International*, *Third Coast*, *Provincetown Arts*, among other periodicals and has been widely anthologized.

Karen Gibson is Director of the WORD Studio and Visiting Instructor of Rhetoric& Communication at St. Lawrence University, in Canton, New York. She has also taught classes at SUNY Potsdam for many years, and has been published in *Blueline*, *The Shawangunk Review*, and *The Explicator*.

Penelope Myrtle Kelsey is associate professor of English and Ethnic Studies at University of Colorado at Boulder. She is of Seneca descent (patrilineal) with familial roots in Pennsylvania and New York. Her book, *Tribal Theory in Native American Literature*, was published at University of Nebraska Press in 2008. Her current research examines Haudenosaunee images of wampum in works by contemporary Haudenosaunee authors and artists and considers their role in traditional knowledges, intellectual transmission, and cultural resurgence in the Iroquois Confederacy.

Alan Steinberg is a Professor of English and Communication at SUNY Potsdam, and has published fiction (*Cry of the Leopard*, St. Martin's Press); poetry (*Fathering*, Sarasota Poetry Press); and drama (*The Road to Corinth*, Players Press). Plays of his have been produced by The Players and Playwrights of Kansas City, The Palladium Theater, the Idaho State Theater

Department, the Atlantis Playmakers, The New Jersey Dramatists, and the Tri-State Actors Theatre, among others. His radio play, *The Night Before the Morning After*, won the national award for radio drama sponsored by the American Radio Theatre. He wrote the libretto for *The Sailor-Boy and the Falcon*, music by Paul Siskind, which was based on Isak Denisen's *The Sailor Boy's Tale*, and which featured Metropolitan Opera star Stephanie Blythe. Most recently, he has won playwriting competitions sponsored by the Dubuque Fine Arts Players and the Vermont Actors Repertory Theatre.

James Thomas Stevens (Akwesasne Mohawk) is the author of eight books of poetry: *Tokinish*; *Combing the Snakes from His Hair*; *(dis)Orient*; *Mohawk/Samoa: Transmigrations*, with Caroline Sinavaiana; *The Mutual Life*; *A Bridge Dead in the Water*; *Bulle/Chimère*; and *of Kingdoms & Kangaroo*, with Nicolas A. Destino. His prose also appears in numerous journals and anthologies. A National Poetry Series Finalist, Gerald Red Elk Scholar, and Whiting Writers' Award recipient, he has taught at Brown University, Haskell Indian Nations University, and the State University of New York at Fredonia. He is on the Creative Writing Faculty of the Institute of American Indian Arts in Santa Fe, New Mexico.

Lisa Tatonetti is an associate professor of English and American Ethnic Studies at Kansas State University where she studies, teaches, and publishes on American Indian literatures with a focus in Two-Spirit studies. She is co-editor of *Sovereign Erotics: A Collection of Two-Spirit Literature* (U Arizona P, 2011) with Qwo-Li Driskill, Daniel Heath Justice, and Deborah Miranda and is currently completing a book project entitled *Queering American Indian Literature: The Rise of Contemporary Two-Spirit Texts and Criticism.*

Susan Ward is a professor emerita of English at Saint Lawrence University. She specializes in Native American literature.

Craig S. Womack teaches in the English Department at Emory University and is the author of *Art as Performance, Story as Criticism*. Recently, he participated in an interactive conversation with Lisa Brooks, Michael Elliot, Arnold Krupat, and Elvira Pulitano, filmed live and later published on southernspaces.org, titled "Cosmopolitanism and Nationalism in Native American Literature: A Panel Discussion."

INDEX